ALL
ROADS

To Mike -

Printed in the United States of America

Cover photo by Greg Benz Photography

Cover design by Richard Aleman

Interior design by Ted Schluenderfritz

LCCN: 2014944520

ISBN: 978-0-9744495-4-8

ALL ROADS

Roamin' Catholic Apologetics

DALE AHLQUIST

ACS BOOKS

ALSO AVAILABLE FROM ACS BOOKS

The Return of Father Brown by John Peterson

The Hound of Distributism edited by Richard Aleman

The Catechism of Hockey by Alyssa Bormes

Jousting with the Devil by Robert Wild

To three men who have walked the road with me:

Nathan Allen, Ted Olsen, and Art Bowman

A man is not really convinced of a philosophic theory
when he finds that something proves it. He is only really
convinced when he finds that everything proves it.

—G.K. CHESTERTON

CONTENTS

INTRODUCTION

Becoming Catholic was the most difficult decision of my life. It was a decision I had to defend at the time I entered the Church and again almost every day since. And it was a decision I have never once regretted.

In this book, I will begin with an unnecessarily long prologue telling the story of my conversion. But the rest of it is composed of mercifully short and hopefully sweet accounts of some of the encounters that happened afterwards, the opportunities where I have had the pleasure of defending the faith that I have embraced. There is always someone or something fighting the Catholic Church, and I have found it nothing less than sublime to give them the fight they are asking for. But while defending the faith provides the exhilaration of battle, it also provides a certain serenity, a peace of mind that comes from having the truth reaffirmed at every turn. "If Christianity should happen to be true," says G.K. Chesterton, "then defending it may mean talking about anything or everything. Things can be irrelevant to the proposition that Christianity is false, but nothing can be irrelevant to the proposition that Christianity is true." Anything and everything. That is what these short meditations are about. The doctrines and teachings of the Catholic Church relate to every conceivable subject, but conversely, every subject, every idea, every issue is a ready opportunity to demonstrate the truths of the Catholic Church. Everything has a way of pointing to the truth. I suppose another way of saying it is that all roads lead to Rome.

Because the universal truth applies to everything, there is often the urge, when engaged in apologetics, to say everything at once. The challenge in trying to make distinct points is to avoid repeating oneself when making other distinct points. You will see that I have failed miserably in that regard. It is almost impossible not to repeat oneself when each point is so intimately connected. You will also note my glorious weakness in quoting my friend Mr. Chesterton to illustrate nearly every point, though sometimes I lapse into quoting the Church Fathers, or even, in extreme cases, Scripture. It is the part of my apologetics for which I make no apology. Also, I have the happy tendency to refer to Chesterton in the present tense. Though my jolly mentor has a better grasp on current events than any other writer I know, I should probably point out that he died in 1936. Timeless truths are the bane of calendar-keepers.

While some of these chapters appear here for the first time, most of them had an earlier, though different form of life in *The Catholic Servant*, *Chronicles*, *Crisis*, *The Coming Home Newsletter*, *Dappled Things* and of course, *Gilbert*—which is the best magazine in the world. My thanks to all of these fine publications. My greatest thanks, however, is to the woman who spends most of her time being my wife and the mother of our six children, but some of her time being my severest literary critic.

Finally, though defending the faith involves taking up arms against any challenger we meet along the road, it is ultimately an act of charity. Our goal is not to crush our opponents but to convert them. We should never forget this goal. Some of the former enemies of the Church have become her most passionate defenders. While I am an unworthy example, it is still an honor to be included in their ranks.

My Road

He was called the "Father of Jesus Rock." Everyone who was an Evangelical or Pentecostal Christian in the 1970's knew who he was. He wrote such songs as "I Wish We'd All Been Ready," "U.F.O." "One Way," "I am a Servant," and "Righteous Rocker, Holy Roller." He was the one who lamented playfully, "Why Should the Devil Have All the Good Music?" He had brilliant lyrical and musical gifts. He could hold an audience in the palm of his hand, easily making them rock with laughter or roll with praise, or making them very quiet and thoughtful.

His name was Larry Norman. And he was married to my sister.

My brother-in-law was certainly one of the most influential people in my life. As a teenager in the 1970's, I, too, wore my hair long and played the guitar and wrote songs. I was also an outspoken Christian, and everyone who knew me knew I was a Christian. I was unafraid to share my faith, unafraid to defend it. I probably was not very good at either. I certainly was not good at living up to it.

Larry not only helped pay for my college education, he provided some fascinating summer employment in his office and recording studio in Los Angeles, which was a long way from my home in St. Paul, Minnesota. With him, I always felt right in the thick of things. And during those interesting summers, I had long talks with him about everything: music and movies and art and love and the world and God.

But his primary influence on me was not those talks or his dynamic personality or that creative intellect or the fact that he was married to my sister or that he was too religious for the rock-and-roll people and too rock-and-roll for the religious people. It was something else. It happened one day when he saw me reading *Mere Christianity*.

"You like C.S. Lewis?" he asked.

With great wit and profundity, I replied, "Yeah."

"Have you ever read any G.K. Chesterton?"

"I've never heard of G.K. Chesterton."

"Chesterton is a lot better than C.S. Lewis. In fact, if you read Chesterton, you wouldn't even need to read C.S. Lewis, because all of Lewis is inside Chesterton."

To me this bordered on blasphemy, but the comment stuck in my head. I soon began to notice references to Chesterton here and there in Lewis' writings. I then discovered that C.S. Lewis had been a confirmed atheist until he read *The Everlasting Man* by G.K. Chesterton. Lewis said that a young man who is serious about his atheism cannot be too careful about what he reads. He called *The Everlasting Man* the best book of apologetics in the 20th century. But it would be four more years before I would actually get my hands on a Chesterton book, and a lot of things changed in those intervening years. Larry divorced my sister, and his career as a Jesus Rock singer began a steady decline. I graduated from college, and in 1981, got married.

My wife Laura and I went to Italy on our honeymoon. She had been born there, and it was nice to have her along since she spoke the language. We were in Rome on a rather momentous day: May 13, 1981, the day Pope John Paul II was shot. We were in the Church of St. Peter-in-Chains, looking at Michelangelo's statue of Moses, when we heard the news. As we walked back to our hotel room, we watched the city transform from utter chaos to an eerie calm. After the sirens died down, the streets became strangely empty, and a silence descended on Rome. It was as if everyone went home to pray. A few days later street vendors were selling postcards of the Pope waving from his hospital bed.

Little did I know that my path to Rome began in Rome. The city amazed me in every way, with the weight of its history and beauty, and with the urgency and significance of what was happening at that very moment. But the farthest thing from my mind was that I would ever become a Catholic. I was only there as a tourist. An outsider. Born and raised a Baptist, I knew my Bible sideways and diagonally. And I knew all the things that were wrong with the Catholic Church. But a seed was planted while I was there; an unlikely seed in unlikely soil. It had nothing to do with the churches I saw or the shrines and holy sites or any of that. It had to do with the reading material I brought with me on my honeymoon: a book by G.K. Chesterton.

People get a good laugh out of the fact that I read *The Everlasting Man* on my honeymoon. What makes it even funnier is that my bride was reading *Les Miserables*. And crying her eyes out. In contrast to her experience, my sensation upon reading my book was the same as that described by Dorothy L. Sayers the first time she read Chesterton: she said it was like a strong wind rushing into the building and blowing out all the windows. It was utterly fresh, and it knocked me over. I knew I had encountered a writer like no other. His words resounded with a splendor of confidence and truth from the opening sentence: "There are two ways of getting home; and one of them is to stay there." In the book, which is a condensed history of the world, Chesterton demonstrates that Christ is the center of history, the center of the human story. He brings together history, literature, mythology, science and religion, and he swats the skeptics who scoff at the Christian claims. "The most ignorant of humanity know by the very look of earth that they have forgotten heaven." Chesterton gave me a completely new perspective of the coming of Christ: a baby, outcast and homeless. "The hands that had made the sun and the stars were too small to reach the huge heads of the cattle." He awed me with his description of the crucifixion, when the darkness descended, and "God had been forsaken of God." And then the resurrection, which was the first morning of a new world, when "God walked again in the garden."

I did not know at the time that Chesterton was a Catholic convert. It was a fact that I continued to avoid as I continued to collect and read books by Chesterton: *Heretics, Orthodoxy, All Things Considered, Tremendous Trifles*, even books with giveaway titles like *St. Francis of Assisi, St. Thomas Aquinas*, and the Father Brown mysteries. I simply could not get enough of this unique writer. I found that there was no subject that he did not address, that he said something about everything and said it better than anybody else.

I could not understand why hardly anyone had heard of G.K. Chesterton, why he was not required reading in the schools, why his sweeping ideas, his energizing wit and his profound insight were not discussed and debated and searched out and savored by everyone.

In 1990, I completed a master's thesis on Chesterton, and that same year I was delighted to learn of a Chesterton conference being held in Milwaukee. I drove six hours from the Twin Cities, and when I walked into the room there were about 20 people sitting in a few rows of folding chairs, listening intently to an

Englishman named Aidan Mackey giving a talk on Chesterton's poetry. I suppose I should have felt self-conscious not only for walking in late but for the fact that everyone turned and looked at me, noticing no doubt that I was about thirty years younger than the next youngest person there. But I did not feel a bit uncomfortable. I immediately knew I was among friends, people who had discovered the same treasure that I had discovered. As I had the pleasure of getting to know these Chestertonians, I was not surprised to find that they were incredibly articulate, morally grounded, and fun loving. But I suppose I was a bit surprised to find that almost all of them were Catholic. It was the first time I had ever met Catholics who could actually explain and defend their faith.

A year later I was back and presenting a paper at their conference, a synopsis of my master's thesis. It was warmly received, and I was soon contributing a regular column to a modest Chesterton newsletter. I invited friends to attend subsequent conferences with me, and as the Midwest Chestertonians continued to tap me to do work for their small group, I had an urge to do even more, to get more people to discover Chesterton. Here was a complete thinker. No holes. No loose ends. His Christian faith, his philosophy, his art, his politics, his economics, his literature and his laughter were all of a piece, truly a seamless garment, and I regarded this neglected literary master as a prophet holding the cure for what ails the modern world. People who had not heard of him and had not read him were simply being cheated. So with the help of some co-conspirators I started the American Chesterton Society, and soon after that helped launched *Gilbert! The Magazine of G.K. Chesterton*. And this all happened before I became a Catholic.

But let's back up a minute.

My father was a Baptist missionary's son. He was born and

raised in the jungles of northeast India, in Assam, among the head-hunting tribes of the Garo Hills. His father was a doctor and a pastor, who not only brought the good news of Christ to the natives but also medical miracles that healed thousands of people. Dr. Ahlquist was a beloved man who was tragically killed in an automobile accident on a mountain road when my father was only 18 years old. My father came back to America, went through college and the navy, and then met my mother at a Baptist church in St. Paul. She was a farm girl who had come to the big city to study nursing. My father became a high school biology teacher, and he and my mother had six children. We went to church four times a week. I was a counselor at a Billy Graham Crusade when I was 14 years old. I lead youth groups and Bible studies and "singspirations." By the time I was in college, I could recite whole books of the Bible from memory. I was active in Inter-Varsity Christian Fellowship in college, and challenged my professors about, well, everything. I even taught a weekly class to other students on Christian apologetics.

But it was while I was in college that I began to feel a burden that would not go away. I was very troubled by the deep divisions within Christianity. I took the opportunity to visit every single church in Northfield, Minnesota, the classic little college town where I was a student. I wanted to see what they were like, and I got a taste of over twenty different denominations (but since this was Minnesota, an undue portion of them were Lutheran.) For the most part, there wasn't much difference, but there was always *some* difference. The most telling event came one Sunday when I attended a "New Testament" church. It was new indeed and was meeting in a temporary facility, an Odd Fellows home. Yeah. There were only 30 people there, a group of maybe 7 or 8 families. But I soon learned that it was the final Sunday that they would be meeting together because the following Sunday they were going to be splitting up into two different churches, not for evangelistic reasons, but because they had a disagreement. This tiny nascent group could not hold itself together, and so one faction was breaking away to form a new church. To me it epitomized everything that was wrong with Christianity. Instead of working out their differences and mending their divisions, instead of uniting in Christ, they splintered off into a still smaller group, with a new name, a new denomination, thus rendering themselves more insignificant and ineffectual in a world that needed Jesus. It was clear to me that though they were utterly sincere and devout in their faith, there was no way that such a show of sincerity or devotion honored the body of Christ. It was division. It was brokenness.

I got married a year after college, and after our Italian honeymoon, Laura and I began to look for a church that we could attend regularly. We soon gave up. Nothing seemed quite right. I eventually became a "lone ranger" Christian. When we had kids, we had "home church." And why not? There was nothing that was done in a Protestant church that we couldn't do at home. We read the Bible, we sang, we prayed, and I sermonized. Once in a while we did attend a church, and had the exact same experience: some scripture, songs and prayers wrapped around a sermon.

Even though my theology was still Baptist, I no longer wished to be known as a Baptist, but simply a Christian. I noticed, too, that the mega-churches in the Twin Cities that had previously called themselves Baptist, had also dropped the word "Baptist" from their names. I also noticed that they were looking less and less like churches. Their "sanctuaries" had become mere auditoriums. But whether they were latent Baptists or blatant Baptists, the fact is, there were still over fifty different Baptist denominations.

In the meantime, I was reading Chesterton. And looking for a place to pray. During the week, I would "sneak" into Catholic churches and kneel and pray, reciting one of the many Psalms that I had memorized, such as Psalm 130: "Out of the depths, I cry to you, O Lord. O Lord, hear my prayer... My soul waits for the Lord. More than the watchman waits for morning. More than the watchman waits for morning."

Here was a sanctuary. Here was a holy place.

I had a brand new problem. I found myself longing for the ancient, historical faith. I had to admit, reluctantly, that Baptists were a relatively recent phenomenon in the history of Christianity. What, I had to ask, was going on during that huge period of time before the Reformation? None of that had ever been explained to me. It had only been explained away. I started to dig into that history, reading the early Church Fathers, and books on the history of the Church. I also read the Catechism, and Chesterton's most Catholic books: *The Thing, The Catholic Church and Conversion, The Well and the Shallows*.

Chesterton describes the three stages a convert goes through. The first is deciding to be fair to the Catholic Church. But there is no being fair to it. You are either for it or against it. When you stop being against it, you find yourself being drawn towards it. Then comes the second step, the fun one. It is learning about the Catholic Church, which is like exploring an exotic country full of strange new animals and flowers that you had never imagined existed. It is fun because there is no commitment, and you can run away anytime you want. Which is what the third step is: running away. You do everything you can to avoid becoming Catholic. You know it is the right Church, and you will not admit it, because admitting it means changing your life forever. Your head is convinced, but your heart is still trying to talk you out of it.

One by one, I had dealt with each of my Baptist objections to Catholicism. Any good Baptist is raised with a subtle and sometimes not-so-subtle anti-Catholicism. The Baptist way could almost be described as a point-by-point reaction against and rejection of Catholicism. We rejected the Pope, the priest, the Eucharist, celibacy, saints, confession, crucifixes, and so on. We identified ourselves by the name of a sacrament we also rejected. Though we insisted on "believer's baptism" and full immersion, we also insisted that it had absolutely no effect on a person whatsoever. It was merely a symbol. The Bible was our final authority in all matters, and we were quite convinced that the Catholic Church deliberately kept its members from reading the Bible in order to keep them ignorant and malleable—which is quite a trick, especially if you can do it for two thousand years.

There is a major hole in the logic of those Christians who protest against the Catholic Church: you cannot use the authority of Scripture to attack the authority of the Church because it was the Authority of the Church that gave Scripture its authority. The hierarchy, the sacraments, the major doctrines of the Catholic Church were all well in place before the Biblical Canon was in place. Centuries in place. And of course it was the Church that authorized the Biblical Canon. Chesterton says he can understand someone looking at a Catholic procession, at the candles and the incense and the priests and the robes and the cross and the scrolls, and saying "It's all bosh." But what he cannot understand is anyone saying, "It's all bosh—except for the scrolls." The Protestants took the scrolls and walked out of the sanctuary. They left the Church behind.

It was a surprise to learn that the Catholic Church, in spite of its reputation among Baptists, is intensely scriptural. Ironically, at any Catholic Mass you will hear far more scripture than at any Baptist service. And it was also my observation that every Protestant sect at some point simply disregards certain Scriptures that are not convenient to its own teachings. Someday I'll make a list.

I will not deal here with all of my objections to Catholic doctrine and how each was resolved, but I must mention one. The first hurdle and the final hurdle for me was Mary. I'm sure it is the same for most Baptist converts to the Catholic Church. Mary represents all the things we object to in one package. She is the pagan remnant in the Catholic faith, goddess worship, idolatry, bigger than Christ in all those prayers and art and music devoted to her, appealing to the ignorant who do not read their bibles, and so on.

My objections to the Catholic view of Mary were deeply ingrained. The first thing that helped me overcome them was reading something that Cardinal Leo Suenens once said when speaking to a group of Protestants. He said, "I'm going to say to you what the angel said to Joseph in a dream: 'Don't be afraid of Mary.'"

I was indeed afraid of Mary.

Do not be afraid of Mary. This is the first step. And it was like the three steps of conversion. I had to start by deciding not to fear Mary but to be fair to her. Then it was a matter of discovering her. Then... running away from her.

The next thing that helped me with Mary was something I read when I went on a retreat to a Trappist monastery in Iowa. (Imagine! Here's a guy who thinks he's running away from the Catholic Church, and he goes on a retreat to a monastery! Though I have never been too bright, I have still always managed to outsmart myself.) In that place of silence and solitude I read how the monks there model themselves on Mary because Mary is the model Christian. She obeyed God's call, she carried Christ within her, and she then revealed him to the whole world. She stayed close to him, she experienced the suffering of his death, the glory of his resurrection, and the coming of the Holy Spirit. We are to imitate her. What she did literally, we must do in every other way. Who can argue with that beautiful image? It is an image worth meditating on every day, which is what devotion is, and why so many have meditated on and been devoted to Mary. They have also fulfilled her prophesy in Scripture by rising up and calling her Blessed.

Next I grappled with the paradoxical but theologically accurate description of her as "The Mother of God." Obviously God created Mary. But Mary gave birth to Jesus Christ, the *Logos*, "the Word made flesh," and it was her flesh. She has the perfect relationship with the Trinity: daughter of God the Father, mother of God the Son, spouse of God the Holy Spirit.

But I still had not completely come to terms with Mary. So I went to another monastery on a retreat. (I was obviously retreating in the direction of the Church.) The priest there looked me in the eye and asked, "Why haven't you converted yet?" No one had ever asked me that question. No one would have bothered before. But this wonderful priest knew it was time to ask the question and time for me to answer it. I followed one of my cardinal rules: When in doubt, mumble. So I mumbled something about Mary. He did not loosen his gaze, but asked, "Do you believe that her soul magnifies the Lord?"

The literal Baptist had never considered that verse literally before. "My soul makes God bigger." I had run out of excuses.

It became clear that every other Christian sect was exactly that—a sect, a section, something less than the whole. I discovered, as Chesterton had discovered, that "the Catholic Church is not only right, but right where everything else is wrong."

The hardest thing I have ever done—and what no doubt delayed my decision—was to tell my parents that I was going to become a Catholic. These were good, Christian people who had raised me to be a man of God. I did not want to make them feel that I was rejecting them, but that it was because they had imbued in me a love of the truth that I pursued that truth to its fullest expression. After that first awkward evening when I broke the news to them, we had many deep discussions about the Catholic faith. They asked a ton of questions, and I was able to answer them all, since I had asked all the same questions myself during my pilgrimage. They did not like all my answers, but they admitted that many of the answers made a great deal of sense to them. My father said to me, "You're telling us things we never knew."

I was received into the Catholic Church on the Feast of the Holy Family in 1997, along with my two oldest children, Julian and Ashley. At the same time, my wife, who had not been a practicing Catholic when we met, returned home to the Church. We have never looked back.

Not long after my conversion, I was invited by Marcus Grodi to be on his EWTN program, "The Journey Home," to talk not only about Chesterton's conversion, but my own. As I walked off the set at the end of the program, the producer came up to me and said, "We should do a whole series on Chesterton." About a year later I was taping the first season of "G.K. Chesterton: The Apostle of Common Sense." My conversion led to a new vocation. I became, as some have said, "The Apostle of the Apostle of Common Sense," and I have had the privilege of traveling the country giving talks on the life-changing writer, G.K. Chesterton. The literary society became a full-time Catholic apostolate with a unique form of evangelism.

Chesterton says, "Becoming a Catholic does not mean leaving off thinking. It means learning how to think." I can scarcely convey how astounding that comment is from someone like Chesterton, who was not exactly a dunce before his conversion. But I discovered first hand that the Catholic faith was not only central to Chesterton's profound thought, it is central to everything.

One of Larry Norman's songs described Jesus as the Rock that doesn't roll. And though the image of Jesus as a rock is a valid one, one of the many metaphors that describe him—the lamb, the lion, the vine, the shepherd, the door—the image of the rock is far more important for the man that Jesus himself named the Rock: the Rock upon whom he would build his Church. Peter is truly the rock that doesn't roll because Jesus promised that the gates of hell would not prevail against the Church that he built on Peter. There is only one true Church. Everything else that calls itself a church is something that has separated from it. Everything else is a splinter. You cannot call thousands of different denominations "The Church." You cannot even call fifty different Baptist denominations "The Church." You can only look to the Church that they all left behind. We have lived through five hundred years of the Reformation. It is time for the Reunion. Lord, hear our prayer.

I did have a reunion of sorts with Larry Norman. After a twenty-year silence, we reconnected over the phone and through e-mail. I interviewed him for *Gilbert*. And when I was on a speaking tour in California I got together with him for just a few minutes. He was very ill. He expressed his awe at my accomplishment in helping lead the Chesterton revival. I told him he created a monster that day he told me to read G.K. Chesterton, and I thanked him. We said "I love you" to each other and good-bye. Less than five months later he was dead. Grant him eternal rest, O Lord. To quote one of my favorite of his songs: "I hope I'll see you in heaven."

Chapter One

A PAINFUL LITTLE LESSON
ABOUT THE LAST JUDGMENT

The first shall be last. The last shall be first. So we are going to start this book with the Last Things: Death, Judgment, Heaven, Hell. Get the unpleasantness out of the way right now.

I will tell you something that once got me thinking quite earnestly about the Last Judgment. It was an experience with sudden death. Not my own. Not quite. It was my computer that died. But a lot of me was in it. And as you probably have surmised, most of it was not "backed up," especially what was most important to me.

It could have been one of those opportunities to launch into a meditation on the meaning of technology and the complications we have created for ourselves in our attempts to make life easier, but such musings were not what occurred to me. What struck me was death and judgment.

I had not prepared for death. I was not properly "saved," as it were. And then: boom.

It was quite horrible, staring into the vast abyss. There was the loss of information, the loss of hard work, the loss of creative endeavors, the loss of images, the captured memories of my experiences, the loss of a collection of ordered things that I had been putting together for a long time. Ordered, that is, but for the fact that I hadn't prepared for their sudden annihilation. I had not prepared for sudden death. In a flash, everything was lost. And what did I have left to show for it? Nothing.

The death of my computer would only have been a minor inconvenience if I had maintained the simple discipline of regularly backing up my work and saving it elsewhere. But a little procrastination here, a little carelessness there, and pretty soon a little became a lot. And what a price to pay as a result. The geeks get rich off this bad behavior.

But it made me think about larger and more important things than my scattered words. It occurred to me that when we fall into bad habits, we can fall far indeed. Finding easy excuses to skip Mass on Sunday, putting off Confession, neglecting our prayers, and soon we are setting ourselves up for a devastating crash. When the wrong sort of pattern develops in our spiritual lives, we slowly start justifying a lie here and a foul word there. Eventually we are in a rut of covetousness and hate, wondering why things are so much better for everyone else and so rotten for ourselves. All the while there is the nagging voice of our conscience telling us to take care of these things, to pay attention, to watch and pray. But we actively ignore that voice. We develop what the Old Testament calls "a hardness of the heart." It is the deadly sin of sloth, the idea that we don't need to do the things that we need to do because we seem to be doing so well without doing them.

Then, without warning, without preparation, our body stops working. We are dead. What then? Is our soul retrievable? That is the question. How far had we fallen from God's grace during those days of neglecting our soul? Are we ready to stand before the Judgment Seat of God?

We could learn something about this dreadful but certain potentiality from our computers. We could make the gigantic effort to do the simple tasks. We could learn to be ready for the end so that death itself is nothing but a minor nuisance, as we are preparing our souls for eternity. We need to be disciplined in our spiritual life.

The lack of discipline is a lack of discipleship. The word "disciple" means "student." A student has to be disciplined, has to follow the rules, has to repeat the same actions, has to pay attention, has to study closely and carefully, and has to be faithful. Discipline means faithfulness. And faithfulness brings joy, a joy that no one can take from us. It means being ready to meet anything that happens, but especially being ready to meet Christ. At Christmas we sing, "O Come all ye faithful, joyful and triumphant." If we are faithful, then we will certainly be joyful and triumphant when we meet Christ face-to-face.

Chapter Two

A HAPPY LITTLE REFLECTION ON HELL

The fear of death is universal and quite natural. In fact, Chesterton calls the fear of death common sense, "a coarse and pitiless common sense." We all know we are going to die, and we all hate the fact that we are going to die. Death is something rotten. It is the failure of the flesh. In fact, Chesterton often used the fear of death to make people better appreciate life. When someone said that life was not worth living, Chesterton took out a gun and offered to shoot the person. Suddenly, for some reason, when you're staring down the barrel of a gun, life *is* worth living! Life is good. Life is precious.

While the fear of death is universal, the fear of damnation is more personal, more individual, because the fear of damnation is the voice of our conscience. It is calling ourselves into judgment. It is the inescapable sense that if we were to get the judgment that we really deserved, it would not be pretty. Justice is something we all want when we feel we have been wronged. But justice is something we really don't like to think about the rest of the time, which is most of the time. Our fear of damnation is really only a deep realization that God is just.

Just as Chesterton uses the fear of death to evoke a deeper appreciation of life, he uses the fear of damnation to create a deeper appreciation of salvation. The fear of damnation is usually portrayed as something very negative, but Chesterton does not hesitate to portray it as a very positive thing. In his book on St. Francis of Assisi, he writes:

> A very honest atheist with whom I once debated made use of the expression, "Men have only been kept in slavery by the fear of hell." As I pointed out to him, if he had said that men had only been freed from slavery by the fear of hell, he would at least have been referring to an unquestionable historical fact.

It was the fear of hell that freed the slaves. Slaves were not afraid of hell, but slave-owners were. Thomas Jefferson fretted about the fact the newly formed United States of America, founded on freedom had not freed the slaves. He was worried, he said, "because God is just."

Throughout history, the saints and other lovers of justice have preached for the reform of society, to make it more just, to make it less hellish for the poor and the oppressed. They used simple words about good things like bread and land and children and churches, and simple words about bad things like crime and sin and death and hell.

They were preaching to the smug and the self-satisfied, to those who abuse every one of God's gifts, including the gift of language, to create philosophies that rationalize away religion. Chesterton calls these the philosophies of "unfathomable softness." They have forgotten God certainly. But their big mistake before that, is that they have forgotten hell.

When you forget hell, it means you have forgotten the larger reality outside of yourself. You have collapsed into egoism and self-centeredness. Hell is separation from God. And just to make it worse, hell is being stuck with only yourself.

Hell, of course, is always portrayed as fire, but when you forget hell, you freeze. (Which is probably why Chesterton compared Scandinavia to hell). Chesterton says, "The place where nothing can happen is hell." You cannot act. You are frozen. That is why hell is symbolized by chains, and heaven is symbolized by "wings that are free as the wind."

But ironically, you cannot *act* in this world, unless there is a hell. You cannot act unless you know that your actions are significant, eternally significant. You cannot act unless there are consequences for your actions, whether they are good or bad.

In other words, without hell, there is no free will.

We were made for heaven, but we are not forced to go there. Chesterton says that it is a fundamental dogma of the Catholic Faith "that all human beings, without any exception whatever, were specially made, were shaped and pointed like shining arrows, for the end of hitting the mark of Beatitude." But the shafts of those arrows, he says "are feathered with free will." And with free will come "all the tragic possibilities of free will."

The most tragic of the tragic possibilities is eternal damnation. The Church has always tried to emphasize "the gloriousness of the potential glory," but it also has to "draw attention to the darkness of that potential tragedy."

There is, however, a creeping error within Christianity, even among Catholics, called Universalism, the idea that everyone will go to heaven no matter what. This is clearly contrary to the teaching of the Church, and yet we see in many places an increasing resistance to talk about hell and the "tragic possibilities" that accompany the glory of free will. The Universalists have done the Protestants one better. The Protestants reduced the scheme of salvation to "faith alone," but the Universalists have dumped even faith. It is inclusiveness taken to the extreme.

But human dignity depends on the doctrine of free will. Chesterton says that another name for free will is moral responsibility: "Upon this sublime and perilous liberty hang heaven and hell, and all the mysterious drama of the soul." The drama of the soul is this amazing possibility that "a man can divide himself from God." But even more dramatic is that a man can be reconciled to God. It is not logical—or theological, for that matter—that we can be reconciled with God if we cannot be separated from him.

Hell is not a subject to be avoided; it is a place to be avoided. Not thinking about hell is a great danger. We might even fool ourselves into thinking there is no hell. But thinking about hell is a very good idea. It is a good way to keep ourselves out of it.

Chapter Three

BORED WITH HEAVEN

A long time ago, when I was in graduate school, I took a class on Atheism. I thought it would be a good opportunity to find out what the opposition was up to. It turned out to be a fascinating affair with some invigorating discussions about some very mediocre books. The dozen or so students in the class represented the whole spectrum of religious belief, from the ardent atheist, to the vague agnostic, to the sincerely seeking Jew, to the Congregational minister struggling with his faith, to the quietly questioning Methodist, to the lapsed Catholic, to the devout Catholic. I was the token Evangelical Baptist in the class, who irritated everyone else by always quoting the Bible or G.K. Chesterton. So I wasn't much different then from how I am now, except that now I have the Church Fathers and the Popes as additional source material with which to irritate people. And I quote Chesterton even more.

One student that I especially recall was a former Benedictine monk, who had drifted somewhere east in his beliefs though nowhere definite. No longer a practicing Catholic, he was now a practicing homosexual. He had strong opinions against many things, but I never heard him say what he was in favor of. He had what you might call a dogma against dogma.

In one of our discussions the subject of heaven came up. He said that heaven sounded boring to him.

It was a comment that I have meditated on for over twenty-five years.

How could anyone not hope for heaven? If there is not an ultimate purpose to our existence, why should we bother to do things such as, well, paying money to take a graduate course on atheism? Does getting a graduate degree give a higher meaning to meaninglessness?

Being afraid of hell makes some sense, but how could anyone be afraid of heaven? Are they afraid that it might not provide the pleasures that they think are pleasures? Or do they already have such a dim view of pleasure that they cannot imagine an eternity of delight? Have they already tired of their pleasure? Does their pleasure give them no pleasure? Have they conceded that the things they have pursued are not worth pursuing, because they are not worth having forever? But then why can't they give up those things now? Do they want them only because they can throw them away?

If I may be irritating and quote Chesterton: "All this tendency to get tired of things is itself a part of our imperfection in this world, and if we were perfect, we should not tire of perfection."

If I may be further irritating and quote the Bible: "All is vanity." It is the famous phrase from the Old Testament book of Ecclesiastes, the words of the man who tried everything and found it all empty.

And now I will quadruple the irritating effect by quoting Chesterton quoting the Bible:

> There are two alternative things that men generally mean when they say they have found all the world vanity. One is that they believe so ecstatically in the worth of something beyond the world they see, that this world is comparatively worthless. The other is that they believe in nothing beyond the world they

see, and find that world intrinsically worthless. They are the direct contrary of each other, like many people who say the same thing. To the first sort of man the colours of paradise are so vivid that against them green grass looks grey or red roses brown; to the other all possible colours are prejudged as colourless. The former only dismisses this life because it is short; that is, because there is so little of it; but by this very doctrine of the soul he obviously wants more of it. The latter is intrinsically weary of life, and would presumably be still wearier of immortality.

Chesterton has perfectly described the difference between a clear Catholic thinker whose fiery faith is a bright light and an empowering hope—and my melancholy classmate whose faith has faded into gray and whose hope has been utterly extinguished. Unfortunately, this poor fallen Catholic monk epitomizes a society that has stumbled into the rut of passivity. We barely bother to pursue pleasure anymore, but we still expect to be entertained.

Heaven will not be a passive experience. Loving and praising God will not mean sitting around and waiting to be amused. We will actively be doing what we were made to do, without the fog of the Fall, without any doubts about what else we could be doing instead. It will mean satisfaction without satiation and joy that is endless. Excitement is simply not a very adequate word for it, but I think all of our God-given senses will be operating at their full capacity, in a wonder of harmonious perfection and fulfillment without weariness. That is the point. Eternal pleasure is also eternal peace. When we pray for the dead, we pray that they will have eternal rest. Jesus, when he calls us in the Gospels, says, "Come to me, all you who are weary…and I will give you rest." In this world, our labors have made us weary, but so have our pleasures. And the pleasures that do not please God have become heavy burdens for us to bear. Jesus calls us to lay those burdens down. He has something better for us, something that even in the glimpses we have been given is overwhelming to us in our present and fallen state.

We should think about Heaven a little more. Not because we can imagine it, but because we cannot.

Chapter Four

THE OTHER PLACE

The people who scoff at the Catholic belief in Purgatory are usually the same people who will wait in line 24 hours for concert tickets. And they will fail to see the irony.

Dorothy L. Sayers said that the loss of the doctrine of Purgatory has been "a great loss in understanding and charity and has tended to destroy our sense of the communion between the blessed dead and ourselves."

But Purgatory is making a comeback. Not that it ever went away. But ever since the Reformation when the doctrine came under attack, Purgatory, along with priests, had to go into hiding for a time.

"Puritanism struck the sinister note," says Chesterton, "by preserving hell and abolishing purgatory." It replaced the God who saves souls with the God who damns them.

But now that the fabric of Protestantism is almost completely frayed, Protestants have not only lost their obsession with the Purgatory they do not believe in, they have even stopped thinking about the Hell they *do* believe in.

The common Protestant objection to the doctrine of Purgatory is that it is not scriptural. Just as Chesterton says that he never realized how much sense Christianity made until the anti-Christian writers pointed it out to him, I never realized how scriptural the Catholic Church was until I examined the claims of the anti-Catholics who had assured me that the Catholic Church contradicted the Bible. Shocking that the Bible should turn out to be such a thoroughly Catholic document. And once we understand the reason and reality of Purgatory, it is amazing how many references to it suddenly appear throughout the scriptures. Besides the ones that should be (painfully) obvious, like Matthew 12:32; Luke 12:47-48, I Corinthians 10:3-17, II Corinthians 5:10 (look them up), there are lots of other verses that I have always known but never really thought about before (and some that I did not know; I guess they slipped by me somehow). For instance:

> In this you rejoice, though now for a little while you may have to suffer various trials, so that the genuineness of your faith, more precious than gold which though perishable is tested by fire, may redound to praise and glory and honor at the revelation of Jesus Christ. (I Peter 1:6-7)

> Beloved, do not be surprised at the fiery ordeal which comes upon you to reprove you, as though something strange were happening to you. But rejoice in so far as you share Christ's sufferings, that you may also rejoice and be glad when his glory is revealed. (I Peter 4: 12-13)

> Those whom I love, I reprove and chasten; so be zealous and repent. (Revelation 3:18-19)

Although Dorothy L. Sayers never became Catholic, she recovered the Catholic belief in Purgatory because she translated Dante. If you are not able to translate Dante yourself, I recommend reading Sayers' translation of the *Purgatorio*, especially her penetrating commentary and footnotes. The *Inferno* gets all the attention, but Sayers found the *Purgatorio* to be her favorite because it was much more subtle. Dante describes Hell as an abyss and Purgatory as a mountain. The vivid images provide the meaningful distinction between the two. The former leads away from Heaven, the latter leads toward it. And that is the important point about Purgatory: it leads to Heaven.

Purgatory is a temporary state. It is not an eternal alternative for those who were too good for Hell, but not good enough for Heaven. It is the penultimate stop before Paradise for those whose souls are indeed saved. It is a place of preparation, of purgation, of scrubbing our souls clean so that we can see God. Blessed are the pure in heart, for they shall see God.

But because it is not a destination, it is worthwhile to point out that that our goal is not to get into Purgatory. We should be setting our sights and all our hopes on Heaven, on perfect communion with God. We are not supposed to aim below the target.

While Dante's book on Purgatory is born of the fire of his creed and his imagination, a more factual account of Purgatory can be found in the writings of another Italian. St. Catherine of Genoa was a contemporary of Christopher Columbus and from the same town. She came from a noble family but wanted to become a nun. She was married off, however, against her desires, to a member of another rich family. Her husband abandoned her and took up a mistress with whom he had a child. A plague struck Genoa and one-third of the population died while many of the people, especially the rich, fled. St. Catherine stayed and started a hospital. Her renegade husband lost his fortune and came to her to ask forgiveness. She took him in, along with the mistress and the child, and they worked for her in the hospital. She also founded a religious order. Besides all that, she had visions of Purgatory. In her plain and placid descriptions, she paints a different picture than what the parodies portray. It is not about souls in agony, but about drawing closer and closer to the pure love of God. There is suffering only because the soul is still not yet in full communion with God. But that is suffering. And the process of drawing closer to God actually begins here and now.

Besides our own purgation, there is the other strange and surprising role that we play on this side of the veil. Besides looking after our own souls right now, we are called on to pray for the souls in Purgatory. This is an act of charity. And praying for the dead has the salubrious effect of making our own souls better prepared for death, and for eternal life.

St. Paul tells us to weep with those who weep and rejoice with those who rejoice. We usually take this to mean expressing different kinds of sympathy according to the different kinds of emotions and experiences of our friends and neighbors. But we actually do both things at once when we pray for the souls in Purgatory. We suffer with them and rejoice with them as they experience what both St. Catherine of Genoa and G.K. Chesterton call "the fiery love of God."

Chapter Five

PROPHETS TRUE AND FALSE

Why do so many people read horoscopes, go to fortune-tellers or palm-readers, mess about with tarot cards, maybe even animal guts, or, if they're feeling highfalutin, attend talks given by futurists? And yet, why do so many people, often the same people, neglect to read the prophets, that is, the true prophets, such as those found in the Old Testament?

It has to with that pesky problem of free will. Most of our future is up to us. Most of it depends on what *we* do, not on the position of the planets or the length of the creases inside our hands. There are, of course, things that happen to us that we cannot control, but those are precisely the things that we will never know about until they happen. They are the things we cannot predict. The most important question about the future is not what will happen, but what will we do when those spills occur? That answer is entirely up to us.

G.K. Chesterton said: "I know as much about the future as you do, which is nothing." But in spite of being no fortune teller, he was still very much a prophet. Was and is. Over a century ago, he mused, "We are learning to do a great many clever things... The next thing we are going to have to learn is not to do them." He saw that greater technology, which meant greater comforts and conveniences, would also mean more ways to kill people. He predicted that "the march of progress" would lead through birth control, abortion, infanticide, and euthanasia. And he prophesied the following: that the next great heresy would be an attack on morality, especially sexual morality; that the decline of the family would leave us helpless before the power of the state; that "freedom of religion" would mean that no one would be allowed to discuss religion; that if we should try to talk about God as a reality, the modern world would try to stop us any way it could. He was right about all these things and more.

But when a prophet describes the future, it is not a fixed portrait of what must happen no matter what happens now, but a clear picture of what will happen *because* of what is happening now. The prophet takes no pleasure in being right. In fact, he would rather be wrong, that is, he would rather that his prophecies were unfulfilled. He is merely describing what will happen to us if we continue on our current course. He is the one whose sometimes urgent duty it is to point out to the present occupants that their building is on fire and that it would be a good idea to take some sort of action to prevent getting badly singed or perhaps even to procure some means to attempt to extinguish the flames, or at absolute minimum, to flee.

The plea of the prophet is: Repent! Stop! Turn back! You must not continue on this road to ruin, this path to destruction! You are on your way to hell. But it's not too late. You can still change direction. You can still go the other way instead. To Heaven.

Or, as the prophet Isaiah says: "Seek the Lord while he may be found. Call upon him while he is near. Let the wicked forsake his way, and the unrighteous man his thought, and return unto the Lord. And He will have mercy and abundantly pardon."

The doom and destruction described by the prophet, the misery of desolation and despair, is not inevitable. It is a scenario we can avoid. But instead of responding in a positive way, we have too often ignored the prophet because he is describing a future we simply do not want to hear. But what exactly is it that we do not want to hear? It is not the final outcome that troubles us, because that seems too far off. No, it is the message about right now, the part about repenting, about changing our lives, about changing our behavior, that we do not want to hear.

We want fortune-tellers to tell us fortunate things. We want to win without placing a bet, be rewarded for not working, sin without suffering the consequences, and get to heaven without dying. We want someone to tell us that everything is going to be just fine.

This fluffy fatalism is not only an attack on free will, on personal responsibility, but on our human dignity. It degrades honest work and defies justice and good order. It is the opposite of faith. It is not trusting God; it is tempting God. It is one of the temptations with which Satan confronted Christ in the desert: Do whatever you want. Nothing bad will happen to you. God will take care of you no matter what you do.

Don't let the devil whisper any fortunes in your ear. God will take care of us only when we do the right thing. And one of the right things to do is to repent of the wrong things.

Do you really want to know the future? Death, Judgment, Heaven, Hell. Are you ready? The future usually comes sooner than we expect.

Chapter Six

A TIME TO BE BORN, A TIME TO DIE

Birth and death, those two rather notable events in everyone's life, never seem to come at a very convenient moment. I'm talking about convenient for everyone else. In a world that worships convenience, in a world that serves the clock, nothing is more upsetting to the schedule than someone being born or someone dying. Everything has to stop to acknowledge that a new soul has either entered the world or left the world. And that's the way it should be.

There is something that makes us not only stop and think, but also stop and give reverence, whenever we are touched by a birth or a death. Though the birth of a baby is a wonder that cannot be fathomed, as a new set of eyes suddenly gazes with astonishment at the universe, there is something even more profound when those eyes close at the end of a life.

G.K. Chesterton says, "There will always be religions so long as certain primeval facts of life remain inexplicable and therefore religious. Such things as birth and death and dreams are at once so impenetrable and so provocative that to ask men to put them on one side, and have no hopes or theories about them, is like asking them not to look at a comet or not to look out the answer of a riddle." The dead man is always sacred, even to an atheist: "It is a strange and amusing fact that even the materialists who believe that death does nothing except turn a fellow-creature into refuse, only begin to reverence a fellow-creature at the moment that he has been turned into refuse."

As I was on my way to a funeral just a few days before Easter, it suddenly occurred to me why Christmas is more popular than Easter. Never mind that Christmas is easier to commercialize than Easter. Christmas is about a baby being born. Everyone can understand that. Easter is about death and resurrection. No one can understand that. Death, says G.K. Chesterton, "is a distinctly exciting moment," but it belongs entirely to the dead person. Even though we have all encountered death by having the experience of burying someone we love, none of us (at least nobody that I know) has had the experience of being the one that has died. Nor have any of us experienced resurrection. Though death is a thing we are sure of (even if we don't want to think about it), resurrection is a thing we can only hope for (which is why we should think about it).

In Ecclesiastes, we are told that it is better to go into the house of mourning than into the house of mirth, "for herein lies the end of all men, and the living will lay it to heart."

This is to take nothing away from the joy of celebrating a birth. Or even a birthday. Chesterton says, "A man's birthday reminds him that he is alive, when his immediate affairs would only remind him that he was at work or at play, in business or in debt." The point is, even though we celebrate life and enjoy life, it is a good exercise to remember that we must die. *Memento Mori*. It makes us live better. Not recklessly, but religiously.

It is by preparing for death that we prepare for resurrection.

During his brief earthly ministry, Jesus raised several people from the dead. The most famous was his friend, Lazarus, who had been dead and in his tomb for four days. It was this dramatic miracle that inspired the religious leaders in Jerusalem to start looking for a way to kill Jesus. A rather strange reaction to something so wonderful.

The Bible tells us that after he had been raised from the dead, Lazarus had supper with Jesus six days before the Passover. But what happened to Lazarus after that? For the answer, we have to go to early Church history, which is largely tradition. That tradition tells us that Lazarus eventually traveled to Cyprus and lived in the town known as Kition (or Larnaca) for 30 years. While he was there he was visited by the apostles Paul and Barnabas, who ordained him as the first bishop of Kition. Lazarus died at the age of sixty and was buried in a sarcophagus at Kition with an inscription, "Tetraimeros, friend of Jesus Christ." The word "tetraimeros" is translated the "fourth day," the day on which he was brought back from the grave. But just as Lazarus did not remain in his first tomb, he also did not remain in his second. In 891 the emperor of Byzantium, Leo VI, decided that Lazarus should be buried in Constantinople. To placate the residents of Larnaca for removing their patron saint, the emperor built a beautiful church at Larnaca devoted to St. Lazarus, which is still standing today. But Lazarus also did not stay in Constantinople. His body is now in Marseilles. I don't know when or why it was moved. I suspect it happened during the Crusades, when lots of things got moved around, including really good relics. At any rate, Lazarus doesn't seem to be able to stay in whatever grave he is given. I believe he will also not stay in his present grave.

Lazarus is an important symbol. He is a mortal man who came back to life. He represents the ultimate gift that God has given to us: victory over death.

There was one person who found the image of Lazarus to be especially poignant, for on the day G.K. Chesterton was received into the Catholic Church, he wrote a poem that ends with the lines:

The sages have a hundred maps to give
That trace their crawling cosmos like a tree,
They rattle reason out through many a sieve
That stores the dust and lets the gold go free:
And all these things are less than dust to me
Because my name is Lazarus and I live.

Chapter Seven

ALONE

He is probably one of the most misrepresented and misunderstood figures of the 20th century. He is vilified by many conservatives and traditionalists for having ushered changes into the Church, particularly the New Mass, and he is therefore held responsible for all the abuses, liturgical and otherwise, that have chased many of the faithful from their pews over the last five decades. But he is also viciously attacked by the liberals and so-called progressives for maintaining the teaching of the Catholic Church in the face of a torrent of social change.

He had a fitting name: Giovanni Battista Montini. John the Baptist. He was a prophet who prepared the way for one who came after him. He would decrease and the one after him would increase. Indeed, he is now almost totally obscured by the charismatic, media star who followed him. But he is also obscured by the jovial, folksy pope who came before him.

Pope Paul VI was a voice crying in the wilderness.

When he was Cardinal Archbishop of Milan, he was watched closely by only a few Vatican observers. He'd been a career churchman, a secretary to bishops, a diplomat, and a scholar. One young priest who followed his Cardinal Montini's career in those days said, "He seems to walk with a great vision no one else sees." And an old priest mused that Montini always had an air of tragedy around him.

When he was elected Pope after the death of John XXIII, he took the name Paul to indicate that he wanted to have a missionary outreach and to expand the Church. He oversaw the completion of the largest Church council in history, which had been called by his predecessor. He enlarged the College of Cardinals to include wide representation stretching across the earth. He was dedicated to Christian unity, issuing an encyclical on Ecumenism, and meeting with the Archbishops of Canterbury and the Eastern Orthodox churches. He desired to make the Mass more accessible, and while he saw the need for the use of the vernacular in the liturgy, he never wished to do away with the use of Latin. Yet some of his own bishops defied him by opposing the liturgical changes he introduced.

And when a panel of Cardinals and bishops came to him recommending that the Church relax its restrictions on the use of contraception, the Pope found himself alone. He was abandoned by everyone around him. And when he issued the encyclical, the whole world erupted with ridicule and outrage.

A tragedy worthy of Shakespeare? Well, sort of. I once met Shakespeare. Not William Shakespeare, he's been dead over 400 years. It was Frank Shakespeare that I met, former American ambassador to the Vatican. He told me about the time he first met Pope Paul VI. When he walked into the room where the Holy Father received him, Frank Shakespeare was startled to find a very small, sad-looking man who looked like he was carrying the weight of the whole world on his shoulders. The future ambassador said he seriously had the urge to go over and put his arm around the Pope and say, "It's okay…" Tragedy was in the air. The reason for the Pope's great sorrow was that the Encyclical *Humanae Vitae* was facing almost universal scorn and condemnation by the world, including many people within the Catholic Church.

The Holy Father had upheld the truth, upheld the teaching of the Church. He had gone against the tide and was paying an awful price. The rest of the world wanted sex without consequences. But sex without consequences... has consequences. And the Pope knew it, and since then he has been proved right a million times over. All of his predictions about birth control leading to divorce, leading to abortion, leading to perversion, were absolutely correct, but no one listened at the time.

G.K. Chesterton said "A dead thing goes with the stream. Only a living thing can go against it." Pope Paul VI was almost the only living thing in the world in 1968.

Ironically, the strides he made in Christian unity were undone not by disputes over Christian doctrine, but by his upholding Christian morals. It all came down to that one issue of contraception. One-by-one the rest of the churches in the world caved in to the world. They tried to say that birth control was a private matter. But morality is always a public matter. When condoms are handed out in public schools, we don't sound very convincing when we try to argue that it is a just a private matter. When "a right to privacy" is used to defend abortion on demand as a method of birth control, paid for with tax dollars, there is nothing private about it. Our society is crawling in the filth of forgetfulness. The world did not listen to Pope Paul VI. And now it does not remember what he said.

Attacked by both the left and the right, the pope seemed to withdraw. There was no longer any evidence of a missionary zeal. When he was not being defied, he was being ignored. Some say he died of a broken heart.

Now, almost a half-century later, we should rise and honor the memory of Pope Paul VI. He suffered enormously for the faith. In the face of unbelievable opposition, he courageously defended the Church's teachings and he accurately warned against all the evils that have come to pass when almost everyone at the time ridiculed him. He is a model of the voice crying in the wilderness. Sometimes we will feel very alone in defending the truth. We need to remind ourselves that the truth does not change. It just goes on being true, even if only one person says so.

Chapter Eight

SLIDING SLOWLY INTO EVIL

In the spring of 2005, a disabled woman in Florida was ordered to be starved to death. When I watched the courts rule against saving the life of Terri Schiavo, I did not panic, and yet I had a helpless and frightening feeling. It must have been the same feeling that any faithful Catholic felt back in 1973, when the Supreme Court stopped saving the lives of the unborn with the *Roe v. Wade* decision. It seems that only a few people today really understand the ramifications of the Terri Schiavo case, just as too few understood the ramifications of *Roe v. Wade* over three decades earlier. We have let a monster loose. Things will only get worse, much worse, until we find a way to get the monster back into its cave. In the meantime it will massacre millions. Euthanasia is the flipside of abortion.

Whenever people talked about "how complicated" the Terri Schiavo case was, I could pretty well guess what direction the conversation was going. Even if they did not come out and say what their conclusion was, I was pretty sure what their conclusion was. When they said it was "a private matter, not something for the government to get involved in," I could hear them really saying, "It would be a lot cleaner and easier if they just let the lady die."

We don't like complicated things. We want simple solutions. But nothing is more complicated than life. And nothing is simpler than death.

In a civilized society, however, laws are supposed to protect life. G.K. Chesterton says, "The regulation of traffic in streets certainly rests on an ultimate optimistic philosophy; the doctrine (disputed by many thinkers) that it is a kindness to people to keep them alive." But there have been forces grinding away at this basic principle for the last one hundred years. It began with the "scientific" theory of Eugenics, the early 20th century philosophy of breeding "better" people and preventing procreation among the certain "undesirables." Chesterton warned about Eugenics. He also warned that it would lead to "other evils." We have watched those other evils unfold in the last century moving steadily toward Terri Schiavo's death sentence. In discussing Eugenics, Chesterton says, "Evil always takes advantage of ambiguity," and "Evil always wins through the strength of its splendid dupes." We have watched the advocates of death take advantage of ambiguity in the legal system. We have watched them torture the language as much as they tortured poor Terry Schiavo, and we have watched them foist misinformation on the public and on the courts to turn people into "splendid dupes" who could approve of a horrific crime.

But we have to be careful how we identify the evil. Those who wanted Terri to die did not rush quickly to their decision. They slid slowly to it. Evil is passive. Satan is subtle. Chesterton makes this point very clearly: "Most men now are not so much rushing to extremes as sliding to extremes; and even reaching the most violent extremes by being almost entirely passive." We have become passive by caring only about convenience. But contraception passively leads to abortion. One day we are simply taking a pill. Another day we are tearing apart an unborn baby. One day we are taking out a feeding tube. Another day we are injecting a lethal drug. One day it is a brain-damaged woman. Another day... who? Who's next?

We have found death a convenient solution to the problems of life. It was this same passive mentality of sliding into evil that led a troubled young man in Red Lake, Minnesota, who lived on a steady diet of violent videos and angry music, and dark, defeatist words flickering on his computer screen, to pick up a real gun and start shooting his fellow students and eventually himself. It was a scene that occurred earlier in Columbine, Colorado, and has been repeated elsewhere since. The subtle message of our culture every once in a while becomes shockingly clear: death is the simple solution to a complicated life.

We have become passive because we have lost an idea that is essential to the Catholic faith: the idea of sacrifice. We have lost the idea of the redemptive power, the very virtue of suffering. We are unwilling to suffer. Defending life will always be difficult because it will mean defending suffering. But let us not forget that Jesus asked us to take up the cross, to take the difficult path, the narrow one that leads to life instead of the broad and easy path that leads to destruction.

Chapter Nine

SUDDENLY, THE WHOLE
WORLD IS WATCHING

The news organizations studiously ignored the Terri Schiavo case for years until it was time for her deathwatch, and then the media machine could not keep its unblinking electronic eyes off her. A tragedy is always transfixing, which is why the camera crews arrive at a burning building or a multi-car pile up almost before the rescue crews. But here the tragedy was more complicated. We had the wrenched faces of the woman's parents who were watching their daughter die. We had the heavy bitter face of the husband who had legally arranged for her death. We had the living face of a woman smiling in old photos and videos, while her dying face was now kept safely out of public view. People took sides about who deserved the most pity.

The news organizations gleefully pointed to polls that claimed a majority of people believed that Terri should be "allowed" to die. The people who were fighting for Terri's life were portrayed as a fringe group. This supposed small minority included Pope John Paul II.

It was this Pope, of course, who had described the times we live in as *The Culture of Death*. The argument of the people who wanted Terri dead was the same argument that supports abortion: Terri was an inconvenience. She was a lump of tissue that needed to be removed. She was not fully human. Getting her to stop breathing was just a procedure.

Finally Terri died. But immediately a new deathwatch began for none other than the Pope. He reached the natural end of his life with an "Amen," and the whole world watched. Then the whole world lined up to mourn. Perhaps the Pope was not a member of a fringe group after all.

When he was alive he could be openly ignored. When he was dead, he suddenly had everyone's attention. When he was alive he could be openly defied, when he was dead he suddenly had everyone's respect. The realization of his great accomplishments started to sink in: the fall of Communism and the Iron Curtain, the excitement of the World Youth Days, the comprehensiveness of the many and varied encyclicals, the explosion of new saints, the profound Theology of the Body, and—what I think may be his most enduring legacy and his greatest gift to the Church—the Luminous Mysteries of the Rosary. Less than a decade later he would be declared a saint.

The Pope's beautiful funeral was also a tool for evangelization. We not only saw the glorious pageantry of the Catholic Church, the long reach of its history, the wide reach of its universal truth, but we saw the faces of every nation, class and culture. We saw them all standing together in a peaceful and loving embrace, all facing the same direction. How could anyone who was not a Catholic watch and not feel like an outsider? How could anyone watch and not long to be on the inside of the Catholic Church rather than the outside?

But there were still some people who complained about what Pope John Paul II did not do. They were quiet at first, but then, as speculation grew about who the new Pope might be, they started expressing more loudly their wishes for a Pope who would make the changes that John Paul did not make: women priests, married priests, homosexual marriage, condoms for all. However, it was not really clear who these people represented and what the purpose of these changes was supposed to be. The demands were coming either from anonymous editors who were not Catholic or from Catholics who were not Catholic.

People who did not believe in the Real Presence wanted women to be ordained because women should be entitled to perform the same utterly meaningless rite of Consecration. People who never go to Confession wanted more priests—and why not married priests—to sit in the same confessionals that were avoided on Saturday afternoon. People who have no respect for the vows and the significance of marriage wanted to extend to homosexuals the privilege of making those same hopeless and inconsequential promises. People for whom sex has always been a selfish act wanted the Church to condone their selfishness. Or at least to stop the spread of selfishly transmitted diseases.

And they really imagined that the cardinals were going to elect somebody who would make these changes.

Then a new Pope stepped out onto the balcony of St. Peter's. Surprisingly for some it turned out he was a Catholic.

The groaning from the editorials sounded more than a little desperate. They started sounding like the rantings and ravings of, well, a fringe group. The message was, "Look, we'll tell you how to run your Church; just don't tell us how to run our newspaper."

The Pope does not have to be smart. He has to be right. But Pope Benedict XVI was not only right; he was smart, one of the smartest men ever to become Pope. He explicated the doctrine of the Church with clarity and completeness. And no wobble. But that did not prevent the self-appointed, self-approved ar-bitrators of the archways from declaring their doubts about the whether this lifelong scholar and former professor from the University of Tubingen really had the goods. Chesterton

says, "It is an axiom of the times that experts are always right...
But the Pope is expected to state a case for his infallibility and
the expert is not."

But Pope Benedict had a surprise up his white sleeve. Even
though he watched how his beloved predecessor was a model of
suffering and goodness in the final years and especially the final
days of his pontificate, he decided that it did not have to be a
requirement for every occupant of the chair of Peter to die there.
He realized that leading the world's one billion Catholics required
a physical strength that he no longer possessed. And so he made
a courageous decision that shocked the world: he resigned.

Then came another surprise—the first American Pope (South
American, in this case). The first Jesuit Pope. And the first Pope
to take the name Francis.

Once again, the whole world is watching. The Pope is the
visible symbol of the Catholic Church. *Ubi Petrus, ibi Ecclesia.*
("Where Peter (is), there (is) the Church.") In his marvelous book
St. Francis of Assisi, Chesterton twists this common Latin phrase
in a way that is almost eerily prophetic. He says, "Any number
of philosophies will repeat the platitudes of Christianity. But it
is the ancient Church that can again startle the world with the
paradoxes of Christianity. *Ubi Petrus ibi Franciscus.*" ("Where
Peter (is), there (is) Francis.") Now Francis *is* Peter.

If that bit of seeing into the future is not thrilling enough,
in the same book Chesterton contrasts the scholarly work of St.
Benedict, who carefully protected the culture and the Catholic
faith through the monastic tradition, with the practical energy
of St. Francis, who took the monk out of the monastery and
took the Catholic faith to the streets. In another prophetic
phrase he says, "What St. Benedict had stored St. Francis
scattered." What Pope Benedict stored, Pope Francis scattered.

And what is it precisely that the one stored and the other

scattered? Chesterton explains that perfectly in *The Everlasting Man*:

> What puzzles the world, and its wise philosophers and fanciful pagan poets, about the priests and people of the Catholic Church is that they still behave as if they were messengers. A messenger does not dream about what his message might be, or argue about what it probably would be; he delivers it as it is. It is not a theory or a fancy but a fact. It is not relevant to this intentionally rudimentary outline to prove in detail that it is a fact; but merely to point out that these messengers do deal with it as men deal with a fact. All that is condemned in Catholic tradition, authority, and dogmatism and the refusal to retract and modify, are but the natural human attributes of a man with a message relating to a fact ... The religion of the world, in its right proportions, is not divided into fine shades of mysticism or more or less rational forms of mythology. It is divided by the line between the men who are bringing that message and the men who have not yet heard it, or cannot yet believe it.

Chapter Ten

THE CHALLENGE OF ATHEISM

Why do atheists get so much attention?

I know the answer to that one. It is because normal things don't make the news, only abnormal things make the news. Atheism is abnormal.

Good news does not usually make the news. While we hear about tragic death, and starvation, and homelessness, we do not hear about mourners being comforted, the hungry being fed, and shelter being given to outcasts, which is the daily work of the Church. We only hear bad news. And that is why we hear about atheism. It is bad news.

It is difficult to have a discussion about atheism. Because the main problem with atheism is this: if it is true, then there is nothing to talk about. It means that everything is meaningless, because, as G.K. Chesterton says, "meaning must have someone to mean it." If there is no God, there is no meaning to existence. Ironically for the newspapers, if there is no God, there is no such thing as news. News means that something is newsworthy, that is, that it has significance. But significance has to do with meaning, and there is simply no meaning in anything if we are merely the careless consequence of a mindless, random, unintended ripple in the rolling recklessness of space and time, whatever those categories might happen to include.

A Creator-less creation is a logical difficulty to say the least. Chesterton sums up the problem nicely: "If there were no God, there would be no atheists."

Atheists, of course, hate this argument. And to be fair, since they obviously *are* here, they are entitled to their opinions if not their indignation.

There may be something weirdly liberating in a theology with no *Theos*, but it cannot be considered comforting. What really seems to make no sense is why atheists should care so much about evangelizing. Why bother preaching a godless gospel? What does it matter? Why are atheists so passionate about their unbelief that they want everyone to disbelieve in the same thing they do?

I know the answer to that one. They are passionate because they believe that atheism is true, and truth is something that you cannot keep to yourself. If you have a conviction about something, it compels you to speak out. The atheists have put their faith in something, even if it happens to be nothing, and faith spurs people to action, especially to the action of defending their faith and actively engaging those who attack their faith. The main thing atheists become interested in is attacks upon atheism. Their spineless cousins, the agnostics, might manage to feel insulted by religion and might even toss off a few insults toward religion, but they dare not discount it altogether. They certainly dare not declare whatever it is they do or do not believe. For them, existence is a long exercise in fence sitting.

But the atheist has at least made up his mind, which is an act of courage. Chesterton calls atheism the most daring of all dogmas because "it is the assertion of a universal negative." It is the zeal of atheists that is actually the most admirable thing about them—and in the case of most prominent atheists—the *only* admirable thing about them. They are certainly not admirable for their logic or their common sense; that is, they don't follow their own reasoning to its logical conclusions (which is utter nihilism), and they don't share the basic assumptions of their ancestors or their neighbors. They are constrained by what Chesterton calls "a very sad simplification."

And yet, though they represent a tiny minority of mankind (among both the present and the past), they have gained a peculiar stranglehold on the language. There is an atheistic literary style that has taken over most public discourse. Whenever any human action is named or described, the words that are chosen always suggest that there is no soul in it. Chesterton describes it perfectly:

> Thus they will not talk of love or passion, which imply a purpose and a desire. They talk of the 'relations' of the sexes, as if they were simply related to each other in a certain way, like a chair and a table. Thus they will not talk of the waging of war (which implies a will), but of the outbreak of war—as if it were a sort of boil. Thus they will not talk of masters paying more or less wages, which faintly suggests some moral responsibility in the masters: they will talk of the rise and fall of wages, as if the thing were automatic, like the tides of the sea. Thus they will not call progress an attempt to improve, but a tendency to improve.

The word "Progress" is certainly an atheist catchword. "Progress," says Chesterton, "is Providence without God. That is, it is a theory that everything has always perpetually gone right by accident. It is a sort of atheistic optimism, based on an everlasting coincidence far more miraculous than a miracle."

To the honest and clear thinker, atheism will seem absurd, but the alternative is not some vague thing called theism, or even some general thing called Christianity. And it is not one of the sects that were born out of some adverse reaction to the one Church that is universal. People do not choose between Atheism and Anglicanism. The only real alternative to atheism is Catholicism. That's right. This surprising observation has been made throughout history by St. Thomas Aquinas, Bl. John Henry Newman and, of all people, Herman Melville, the self-torturing Puritan who penned *Moby Dick*. And even more surprisingly, G.K. Chesterton said that if every man lived a thousand years, every man would either be a nihilistic atheist or a member of the Catholic creed. Why is that so surprising? Because Chesterton wrote those words ten years *before* he became a Catholic.

Chapter Eleven

WHAT IS "PRACTICAL ATHEISM"?

I was once asked to give a talk on practical atheism. It sounded like a very interesting topic, even though I really did not know what the term is supposed to mean. That, of course, did not prevent me from giving a talk about it. As G.K. Chesterton says, "I am a journalist and am ignorant about many things, but because I am a journalist I can write and talk about all of them."

I suppose the first definition that might occur to us of what a practical atheist is would be someone who does not believe in God but acts as if he does. After all, most of the actual atheists that we know—certainly the ones I know—would fall into this category. They are generally good, moral, upright people, but they don't have any excuse for it. They cannot really justify their good behavior. They make polite explanations about social contracts and consequential something-or-other, but their arguments are not at all convincing or even comprehensible. Atheists might argue that the evidence that there is no God is that there is so much evil in the world, but they cannot explain why they try to be good. They are not abrasive and obnoxious people like certain well-known loud-mouthed atheists who get a lot of press. And why do they get a lot of press? Because of the simple fact they are unusual. When was the last time you saw a normal person with normal beliefs make the news? Chesterton says, "Atheism is abnormality." A whopping 2% of the population identifies itself as atheist, the same percentage of people (but not the same people) who consider themselves homosexual.

And just as the homosexual cannot stop talking about the normal things associated with sex, such as marriage and children and family, so the atheist cannot stop talking about God and religion. "The atheist," observes Chesterton, "is not interested in anything except attacks on atheism." He wants his non-belief in God to be respected with the same religious freedom afforded to those who believe in God. Unfortunately, this always manages to translate into a restriction on the freedom of believers, so that those who believe in God must not mention God, especially not into a microphone. Just as the homosexual wants to make immorality legal in the hope that it will suddenly not be considered immoral anymore, so the atheist wants to make unbelief the same as belief so that he can enjoy the same sort of "sanctuary" from the outside world that the believer should enjoy inside the Church. Except that the atheist also wants to enjoy the outside world. He is "practical" in the sense that he wants a just and orderly society where everybody obeys the law. He really does want people to behave themselves. In fact, to many people's surprise, there have been some avowed atheists who have taken a public stand against same-sex "marriage" for the simple reason that it is disruptive to society. Morality is useful. But for the atheist, order replaces meaning, and eternity is kept off the calendar.

As I say, that might be the first definition of practical atheism that pops into the mind, but I think the practical atheist is precisely the opposite of the person I have just described.

The practical atheist is not the man who does not believe in God but acts like he does, he is the man who *does* believe in God but acts like he doesn't. He is either afraid to express his belief or does not care enough about it to let it show up in his life. He does not want to talk about his own faith, and he does not want other people to talk about theirs either, because talking about one's faith is usually inconvenient, and almost always uncomfortable, and it might even be dangerous.

The practical atheist is the believer who does not let his faith be seen. And he does not let his faith interfere with his activities.

The practical atheist may believe the Creed and may even recite the Creed in the presence of his fellow believers, but for all *practical* purposes, he is an atheist. He not only does not allow God to influence the way he acts, he does not allow God to influence the way he thinks. He keeps his faith insulated from his intellect. He essentially thinks like an atheist. He does not think about God. He does not think about eternity. This is evident in his work and his play, in his education and his entertainment, in what he buys and what he sells, in what he cries and what he yells, in how he votes, in how he talks, and especially in how he keeps silent. He does not speak up when the things that he knows are wrong are paraded as being right. He prefers the easy alternative to the struggle that truth might demand. It is easy to fall, says Chesterton, it is much more difficult to stand.

I do not have any statistics on how many practical atheists there are, but when I look at what our world has become, when I see the broken families and broken lives and sorrowful souls and the confusion and the rage and the ridiculous ideas that go unchallenged, I suspect that the number of practical atheists is too large a number even to count. They have done their damage by not doing anything.

Catholics do not have a bad reputation for being Catholic. They have a bad reputation for failing to live out the faith they profess. Being Catholic, some would say, is impractical, but the saints have always been known as people who get things done.

Practical atheists do not suffer for their faith, but the world suffers from effects of practical atheism.

Chapter Twelve

THE CHALLENGE OF AGNOSTICISM

I once had a friendly discussion with an agnostic who suddenly tossed off the following question: "Isn't your religious belief ultimately selfish? You just want to get to heaven." As if it is bad to want a good thing. Or as if heaven is a bad thing to want. Or as if charity is really a serpentine scheme to trick God into handing over the eternal rewards. The question by itself is a fairly standard strike that an agnostic will use to put a believer on the defensive. But before I could answer, he went even further. He said that if my faith was truly unselfish, I would be willing not just to die for someone else—since I would be expecting to get to heaven for that—but rather to actually sacrifice heaven on behalf of someone else. That would be truly unselfish.

It sounded—to him, anyway—as an unanswerable challenge. It was, however, quite answerable, but the response involved both correcting his misunderstandings about the Catholic view of salvation and exposing the airy assumptions he was using to support his argument.

It is typical of the agnostic to be selective in his doubts. He questions something perfectly natural to the great majority of mankind—our desire for God—never doubting his own dismissal of the idea that such a desire is itself God-given. And my friend did not question his own strange theological construct wherein God would allow a man to use his own salvation as some sort of bargaining chip. What sort of God does he think would send a man to hell in place of someone else? What sort of God would welcome a devious soul into heaven merely because some "unselfish" soul had given up his own slot? What sort of incompetent judge does he think God is?

The discussion was promising because he seemed at first to be genuinely interested in how I was going to answer the question. But when I began to make my case, he immediately began to interrupt with what Chesterton calls the "cheap and querulous incredulity" of most agnostics. Such an agnostic does not really want to consider the arguments—he wants only to quarrel. He is not genuinely looking for an answer; he wants only to hide behind his questions, especially the questions that pose logical impossibilities; he tries to make up tricks that would somehow cheat God out of his Godliness. For instance, a classic agnostic ploy is to do away with God's omnipotence by asking, "Can God create a stone so heavy that he could not lift it?" It is a loaded question along the lines of "Have you stopped beating your wife yet?" Any answer at all will get you in trouble. But the problem is not that he won't believe your answer; it is that he does not even believe his own question. He is merely playing a game. And while some theological puzzles are amusing and even invigorating to consider, there is nothing constructive about this sort of riddling. The doubter is not trying to build anything, but only destroy what has already been built. Each of his random doubts is a brick he hurls with no concern about seeing the thing he is attacking. It is a kind of theological vandalism.

The agnostic will, of course, deny that he is attacking anything. He says he is merely questioning, merely seeking, always holding open the possibility that he is wrong. Which is to say he is a vandal who knows he might get caught.

Atheism is much more daring than agnosticism. Agnosticism

is safe. Or at least it tries to be. Atheism is a systematic attack; agnosticism is a constant retreat, a duck and run.

Chesterton calls agnosticism "a decision in favor of indecision." And he points out that the word "agnostic" is merely the Greek form of the Latin word "ignorant." He prefers that the agnostic be called by his Latin name.

I continued to try to explain the Christian view of salvation to my friend. I had the joy of pointing out that his clever conundrum has a dramatic solution: someone *did* give up heaven. In fact, someone gave up heaven for *him*, and for everyone else. Christ not only gave up heaven, he descended into hell. What the Christian believes is far more daring than what the agnostic even manages to doubt. While he may feel a bit defiant in scoffing at our creed, ours is the only creed on earth where God himself is a rebel. God put himself to the test, put himself through the emotional agony of the Garden of Gethsemane, and the through the physical agony of Calvary, that led to the cry from the cross where God felt that God had abandoned him. As Chesterton says, "Alone of all creeds, Christianity has added courage to the virtues of the Creator." Christ gave up heaven. Christ suffered like a man. Even doubted like a man. And died like a man.

Heaven is not ours to give up. We have already lost it. We have nothing with which to make any deals with God. Salvation means that God has a plan to give a second chance to the creatures that have defied him. In this amazing plan, he came to his beloved not as an omnipotent God but as a suffering God. And the love with which we might respond to his love is defined in the doctrine and practices of something called the Catholic Church. It is a divine meeting place. An institution of ultimate things. A bearer of divine light across the world and across the generations. The Gospel entrusted to the Church not only sets sinners free from their sin but doubters free from the bad ideas in which they have trapped themselves.

I was explaining to my friend how the Church has been proved right again and again as bad ideas have been tossed like bricks through its stained glass windows. But I only got as far as the ninth century... and then he changed the subject. The faith may be difficult but at least it can be sustained. Doubts are easy, but they do not carry one very far.

Chapter Thirteen

THE CHALLENGE OF ISLAM

We are completely schizophrenic about Islam. We dismiss it, we demonize it, and we dally with it. We go to war against Muslims at the same time we usher tens of thousands of Muslim immigrants into our cities. But the strangest thing of all is how little we actually know about what they believe. That is because most people will do anything to avoid discussing religion and politics, especially in the same sentence.

We always hear about how important it is to respect another person's religion, but this is taken to mean that we just should not talk about it. However, as G.K. Chesterton says, "The way to respect a religion is to treat it as a religion: to ask what are its tenets and what are their consequences. But… we are always saying to a Mormon or a Moslem—'Never mind about your religion, come to my arms.' To which he naturally replies—'But I do mind about my religion, and I advise you to mind your eye.'"

The Muslim takes his religion seriously. If we took our own religion seriously, we would be better equipped to deal with the Muslim. We might understand that Islam is actually a Christian heresy. Islam, of course, came into the world long before the Protestant Reformation. Mohammed drew upon both the Hebrew and Christian Scriptures in writing the Koran. Islam considers Jesus an important prophet, but not the Son of God. (Islam has a very high view of the Blessed Virgin Mary as well.) All of the early heresies were attacks on the Incarnation, sacrificing either Christ's divinity or his humanity. A religion that keeps Christ but leaves out his divinity is a classic heresy.

Chesterton argues that the main thrust of Mohammed's main attack was against the idolatries of Asia. The reactionary response to idolatry is an attempt at "plain theism," which is what Mohammed tried to do. It was a narrowing, like other heresies, but it was different from the other early Christian heresies such as Arianism or Albigensianism because it sprang up on the borders of Christendom and spread outward rather than inward. And it grew and grew. One of the reasons it grew was that it was simple and easy to embrace. Anyone who makes a creed that is going to last longer than ten minutes has to deal with certain basic rules of life. It will always involve gaining something and giving up something. Mohammed's creed did this, and Chesterton says that when the great prophet of Islam "forbade wine but allowed five wives he created a very big thing, which we have still to deal with."

But it was exactly because "their simple creed was suited to everybody, that they wished… to impose it on everybody. It was because Islam was broad that Moslems were narrow. And because it was not a hard religion it was a heavy rule. Because it was without a self-correcting complexity, it allowed of those simple and masculine but mostly rather dangerous appetites that show themselves in a chieftain or a lord." Thus Chesterton explains why democracy will be nearly impossible in a Muslim country. There is no "self-correcting complexity" in its philosophy. It naturally breeds warlords. There is a void "in the heart of Islam which has to be filled up again and again by a mere repetition of the revolution that founded it. There are no sacraments; the only thing that can happen is a sort of apocalypse, as unique as the end of the world; so the apocalypse can only be repeated and the world end again and again. There are no priests; and yet this equality can only breed a multitude of lawless prophets almost as numerous as priests. The very dogma that there is only one Mahomet produces an endless procession of Mahomets." You see, you can't separate politics and religion.

There is one chapter in our history that has been subject to many falsehoods and about which we have been afraid to speak the truth. The Crusades. Most of the falsehoods have been told against Christendom. Yes, there were Christian atrocities, and yes, there were sad examples of Christian sins and failures, but they truly were the exception and not the rule. There was great heroism and gallantry, great courage and valor on the part of the crusaders. And the thing most forgotten is why the Crusades started. Chesterton reminds us that it was Moslem warlords who provoked this war between Islam and Christendom. He points out that the effort of the Crusades was sufficient to stop the advance of Islam, but not sufficient to exhaust it. He says it will always be "a permanent menace" to Christendom. The reason is in the strange contradiction at the heart of Islam itself. "The great creed born in the desert creates a kind of ecstasy out of the very emptiness of its own land." Chesterton suggests that there is similar emptiness to its theology. It insists not merely on the singleness of God but rather on the solitude of God. And that is the source of the permanent problem.

> The Trinitarian God may be an enigma for the intellect; but He is far less likely to gather the mystery and cruelty of a Sultan than the lonely god of Omar or Mahomet. The *heart* of humanity is certainly much more satisfied by the strange hints and symbols that gather round the Trinitarian idea, the image of a council at which mercy pleads as well as justice, the conception of a sort of liberty and variety existing even

in the inmost chamber of the world. For Western religion
has always felt keenly the idea "it is not well for man to be
alone." The social instinct asserted itself everywhere as when
the Eastern idea of hermits was practically expelled by the
Western idea of monks. So even asceticism became brotherly;
and the Trappists were sociable even when they were silent.
For to us Trinitarians (if I may say it with reverence)—to us
God Himself is a society. This triple enigma is as comforting
as wine or an open fireside; this thing that bewilders the
intellect utterly quiets the heart: but out of the desert, from
the dry places and the dreadful suns, come the cruel children
of the lonely God; who with scimitar in hand have laid waste
the world. For it is not well for God to be alone.

Chesterton says that these are the days when a Christian is
expected to praise every creed except his own. He notes that in
19th century historical novels, the Jew and the Moslem is always
portrayed sympathetically, but there is always a strong bias
against the Christian, who is either a fool or a hypocrite. The
Crusades and the crusaders are always used against Christianity.

But the religion that founded our civilization, the religion
that thought Jerusalem so important that thousands of people,
from peasants to kings, died to protect that place though it was
not their home, and spent hundreds of years trying to con-
quer and keep that town—that religion, Christianity, believed
something that the other two did not: that the holiest spot in
Jerusalem and in all the world was an empty grave. And when
Christendom lost that town, something happened. That thing
known as Christendom began to decline.

That decline, whether we want to admit it or not, has continued to this day. But in yet another prophetic insight, Chesterton
says that after all these things, after all these ages, with a wearier

philosophy, with a heavier heart, we have been forced to do again the very thing that the Crusaders were derided for doing. The heirs of the Crusaders find themselves in the Middle East once again. We find ourselves defending the Holy Land once again. Only what was once done with the faith is now being done without the faith. And once again, we find that the Moslem is our enemy.

But we need to examine ourselves and ask ourselves: why is the Moslem our enemy? We are, of course, going to defend our country if it is attacked, but we had better not fool ourselves into thinking that the Moslem is attacking our country because it is Christian. It is a country that has sanctioned 50 million abortions in 40 years, a country that supports a $12 billion pornography industry, a country where condoms are handed out to students in the public schools, and a country that is in the process of legalizing the status of homosexual couples, using the word "marriage."

We are not in a very good position to be self-righteous in any present war or any potential war with the Moslem. He is fighting a religious war. Can we even fight a religious war if we are not religious? Can we win it?

But there is an alternative strategy to going to war against the Moslem. One of the little known episodes of the Crusades was when St. Francis of Assisi traveled to the Holy Land and met with Saladin and other Moslem warriors. According to Chesterton, the idea of St. Francis was simple: that it is better to make Christians than to kill Moslems. Though St. Francis may not have won many converts, he won almost universal respect among the Moslems. The solution to most of the world's problems is the same: we need more saints. If we see that there is a shortage of saints, perhaps that is sign that we need to start being saints ourselves. We need to be streams in the desert.

Chapter Fourteen

THE DIFFERENCE BETWEEN
PAUL AND PASCAL

The Christian faith is centered on the Incarnation, Crucifixion, and Resurrection of Jesus Christ. If any of these three pillars is removed, if any of one of them is not true, the faith collapses: none of it is true. God shares his love by becoming a man, he shares his forgiveness by suffering in our place for our sins against him, and he shares his glory by conquering death itself. The fulfillment of all our hope is eternal life with God.

To the unbelievers and the skeptics, this hope is nothing but wishful thinking. They doubt the Christian message beginning with the historical Jesus and his claims about himself, and continuing with the meaning of his death and above all, the fact of his resurrection. They do not believe it. They do not believe that Jesus is the Son of God. They do not believe that his death on the cross brought the salvation of all mankind from the plague of sin. They do not believe that he rose from the dead.

Throughout the history of the Church, Christian apologists have tried to find logical and compelling arguments to defend these central claims of the faith. Perhaps one of the most dramatic devices for defending the faith comes from the French philosopher, Blaise Pascal (1588–1651), and his argument known as "Pascal's Wager." It is almost confrontational. It puts the burden on the unbeliever. It says, in effect, "Even if we cannot prove that Christianity is true, it still makes more sense to believe it than to doubt it, because if you believe it and it's true, you gain eternal life. If you don't believe it, and it's true, you risk eternal damnation. If you believe it, and it's not true, you don't lose anything: the result is the same if you don't believe it. If you gain, you gain all; if you lose, you lose nothing."

Now there are those who argue that not believing something that is not true is a better approach to the gate, even if the gate leads nowhere. So let's at least have "fun" (which usually means "sin.") Pascal responds that these people do not find the happiness they claim to be seeking in the pleasures of this world. He urges the unbeliever to look at the Christian as an example of the happy man. If you act like a believer—following the teachings of the Church, going to Mass, and so on, the result is that "you will be faithful, honest, humble, grateful, generous, a sincere friend, truthful." You will not suffer the consequences of the "poisonous pleasures." Even in this life you will gain from the faith, let alone the next life. You are really risking nothing and you stand to gain everything.

Sounds reasonable. But contrast this approach with that of St. Paul. He says that if Christ has not been raised from the dead, then Christians are a pitiful and miserable lot. If Christianity is not true, it means that he is a liar, his message is false, his preaching is worthless, we are still in our sins, our hope is vain, and we are being virtuous and long-suffering and faithful for absolutely nothing. "We are of all men the most to be pitied." (I Corinthians 15:14-19)

St. Paul actually states the doubter's argument even more emphatically than the doubter. He apparently doesn't have much use for Pascal's wager, either. But Paul has one advantage over Pascal. He has had a face-to-face encounter with the Risen Christ. He also has the eyewitness accounts of others, even hundreds of others, who had seen Christ in his resurrected and glorified body. He did not need to rely on a fine philosophical argument. He could rely on his own senses, and on the living testimony of others who had seen God in the Flesh, risen from the grave.

As for the doubter, St. Paul does not spend a lot of time coddling their skepticism: "For what can be known about God is plain to them, because God has shown it to them. Ever since the creation of the world his eternal power and divine nature, invisible though they are, have been understood and seen through the things he has made. So they are without excuse." (Romans 1: 19-20)

G.K. Chesterton, in some ways, appreciates both the approach of Pascal and Paul. He believes that there are reasonable defenses for the faith, and that skeptics are better off believing for any number of reasons. Like, Pascal, he points out that it is the doubters who are generally miserable and the believers who are generally happy. The man of faith has an entirely better outlook on life: "It is ludicrous to suppose that the more skeptical we are the more we see good in everything. It is clear that the more we are certain what good is, the more we shall see good in everything."

But he also demonstrates a little of Paul's impatience with the doubter. There is nothing sophisticated about skepticism. Rather, it is immature: "No skeptical philosopher can ask any questions that may not equally be asked by a tired child on a hot afternoon."

Chesterton finds credibility in the claims of Paul and the other eyewitnesses of the death and resurrection of Christ. He finds no credibility in the random and incoherent potshots taken by the doubters who have neither a complete philosophy nor a consistent creed. "The skeptics, like bees, give their one sting and die."

Chapter Fifteen

REASON AND LIBERTY

A dungeon for zombies. That is the image in many people's minds of the Catholic Church. They are quite sure that the requirement for becoming Catholic is to give up reason and liberty. They imagine that when we enter the Church we first check in our brains at the door and then are placed in chains and irons and led about by dour priests who are puppets of the pope, while only outside the walls does reason reign supreme and freedom run free.

But it is quite the other way around. In fact, G.K. Chesterton says that he could explain the whole of the Catholic faith using only "the supreme sacredness and value of two things: Reason and Liberty." These are the foundations of Catholic theology.

The faith is reasonable. Theology is the logic of God. Apologetics is the sword of theology, the sharp edge of reason that slices up the arguments against the faith and makes the critics of the Church very uncomfortable. Swords have a way of making people uncomfortable.

The faith is also the essence of freedom. Every act of faith is an act of freedom. Liberty is the consequence of believing the Truth. As Jesus promised in the Gospel of St. John, "The truth will set you free." Rejecting the Truth, running from the Truth, denying the Truth, makes us slaves, whether to passion, to error, or to doubt.

The assault on these two pillars of the Catholic faith, reason and liberty, began with the Protestant Rebellion. Even if the reformers may have had good intentions, the fact is that Martin Luther with his "Bondage of the Will" and John Calvin with his doctrine of pre-destination paved the way for all the modern philosophies that not only continued the revolt against the Catholic Church, but also revolted against the Protestant churches, against Christianity, against any belief in God at all. They are all the result of the attack on free will. If you take away free will, you will ultimately be left with materialism. Even God is no longer necessary. We are simply part of a vast impersonal machine. Our decisions do not matter because they are not decisions and they are not ours. They are simply part of a mindless process, of mere action and reaction, of sparks and bubbles, of itches and scratches. The ramifications of this attack on free will have been vast indeed. It has led to many schemes of scientific control, it has reduced much of humanity to various forms of servitude, it has produced high-sounding explanations of our behavior that not only excuse us from any responsibility for anything we do but prevent us from doing anything responsible. The attack on free will was, in Chesterton's words, "a particular poison that was ultimately to paralyze the moral activity of man and...turn mankind into a sort of machinery of robots, or dead men walking."

That is why Chesterton calls the Reformation a "colossal but almost casual blunder that...broke the bridge connecting Christianity with humanity." No small criticism. But look at the modern world. We see the fruits of this revolt against the Church, and against free will, everywhere. People are no longer considered sinners but patients. They are no longer expected to do penance, but to be cured. They are no longer encouraged to be saints, but to follow their bliss.

The strangest tendency in modern thinking, according to Chesterton, is the "unnatural and unaccountable pleasure in insisting on the impotence of the human will." Marxists, for instance, insist with a "mysterious relish" that men are utterly fixed or forced by dead economic conditions in what is "proudly called the materialist theory of history, which insists that the march of progress can never be anything but a hunger march." So, too, atheistic anthropologists proclaim with "antic glee…that man was not only a spawn of the mud, but always a slave of the mud," that all our art and religion is the result of appetite. The most obvious thing about "this queer inverted enthusiasm for emphasizing all that was constrained or involuntary about the conditions of men" is that besides being an attack on free will, it is an attack on reason. It is foolishness to try to explain all of humanity, of art, religion, romance, and ritual in such morbidly and moronically simplistic terms. The more sensible, believable, and more reasonable explanation is found in the Catholic Creed, that God created the heavens and the earth, that he visited his creation in the flesh, that he suffered along with his creation, and that ultimately he will judge the living and the dead. That last part is the most logical thing of all. It means that we are accountable for our actions. It means that we are responsible. It means that we have free will.

The world insists on misunderstanding liberty. It thinks freedom means disobedience. But it is the opposite. It means obedience. Disobedience destroys the created order. It banishes us from freedom. Obedience upholds the order and makes everything work the way it was designed to. When we choose to do what we were made to do, we are happy. Wildly happy. The Church has established rule and order, which is reason, and the purpose of reason is to give us the liberty that we were made for. Or, as Chesterton says, "the chief aim of that order was to give room for good things to run wild."

❧

Chapter Sixteen

IS IT BAD TO BE DOGMATIC?

Have you ever been criticized for being "too dogmatic"? Or how about for being simply "dogmatic"? The term "dogma" has become a sort of dirty word in our society. G.K. Chesterton even speculates that the word is used solely for the sake of its sound: "It has a short, ugly sound, like a gruff bark. Indeed, 'dogma' is probably confused unconsciously with 'mad dog.'"

Anyone who takes his religion seriously is considered dogmatic, and is also apparently considered armed and dangerous. But how can one not take one's religion seriously? Certainly there *is* danger involved, for faith is always something of a risk. But isn't it more dangerous *not* to take one's religion seriously? Isn't that playing with fire? It seems to me that someone who does not take his own religion seriously is either a heretic, a hypocrite, or a lunatic.

We never hear of atheists being ridiculed for their dogma, but atheism is the most daring of all dogmas, "the assertion of a universal negative," as Chesterton says, denying the divine at every possible opportunity. The atheist has indeed risked his eternal soul. What could be more dangerous, more reckless, more unreliable than a person who denies the basic principle that God will judge us, who thinks that sin is a mere myth, that guilt is a construct, that rules can be made up and broken without accountability?

The term "dogmatic," however, is reserved for those with positive, not negative dogmas. Yet the person who uses the word dogma as term of contempt will always consider his own strong ideas as if they were facts of science or solid social convictions not subject to dispute. He will not call them dogmas even though he accepts them as dogmas. Chesterton describes him thusly: "Other people's dogmas are dogmas; but his dogmas are only truths."

For example, what do you think of these two ideas: the brotherhood of man and the communion of saints? Most people probably consider the first a truism and the second a dogma. But they are both dogmas.

Chesterton explains that the word dogma is only a general term "for any primary philosophical principle promulgated by the authority of somebody." The authority can either be one that is recognized by a great number of people across a great number of cultures and over a great number of years—the Catholic Church comes to mind as an example—or the authority can be something less universal, more narrow, strictly personal—like oneself. When a person has made himself God, you will find that he is quite dogmatic.

But everyone is dogmatic. It is only a matter of which authority one appeals to.

There are really only two kinds of people, says Chesterton: those who are dogmatic and know it, and those who are dogmatic and don't know it. Unfortunately, it is only those who have a clear and recognizable dogma, one that they can actually articulate, who are cast in a critical light. Obviously it is the people who do not know their own dogma who do the criticizing. They criticize, but they don't argue. They dismiss; they do not engage. That is the great challenge of the believer: to engage those who would dismiss us simply because we know our faith. They disagree with us, but they won't discuss it with us.

Whether or not it is good to be dogmatic depends on what dogma one holds. And that is the crux of the matter. There is always a crux. And no one wants to discuss that. No one wants to discuss the things they really should discuss. As Chesterton says:

> For some mad reason in this mad world of ours the things about which men differ most are exactly the things about which they must be got to agree. Men can agree on the fact that the earth goes round the sun. But then it does not matter a dump whether the earth goes round the sun or the Pleiades. But men cannot agree about morals, sex, property, individual rights, fixity of contracts, patriotism, suicide, public habits of health—these are exactly the things that men tend to fight about. And these are exactly the things that they must not fight about. These are exactly the things that must be settled somehow, and settled on strict principles. Study each of them, and you will find each of them works back certainly to a philosophy, probably to a religion. Every Society has to act upon dogmas, and dogmas are exactly those things that are most disputable. It puts a man in prison for the dogma of the sanctity of property; it hangs a man for the dogma of the sanctity of human life.

So next time someone says to you, "You're being pretty dogmatic…" you can respond: "Yes, I believe something. I believe the Apostle's Creed. I believe in the Father, Son, and the Holy Spirit. I believe in the Holy Catholic and Apostolic Church. What do you believe?" They may choke and sputter, but if they really try to maintain that they do not believe anything, you may want gently to point out to them that their lack of belief is actually a lack of thinking. And if they wish to enjoy such "perfect mental breadth and freedom," as Chesterton says, they had better never think at all. "Thinking is a narrowing process. It leads to what people call dogma. A man who thinks hard about any subject for several years is in horrible danger of discovering the truth about it… It is a terrible thing when a man really finds that his mind was given him to use, and not to play with; or, in other words, that the gods gave him a great ugly mouth with which to answer questions, and not merely to ask them."

Chapter Seventeen

THE BASIS OF CIVILIZATION

"Ideals," says G.K. Chesterton, "are the most practical thing in the world." This is why we still defend the family. This is why we insist on the ideal of marriage as a permanent union between one man and one woman, which creates the only proper setting for bringing new souls into the world, and that this purely natural act should not be interfered with.

The social trends have steadily moved in the opposite direction from this ideal in the last century. It is no longer a matter of a few loud critics getting a little testy at our quaint ideas of morality; we have gone past being attacked to being brazenly ignored. But if the society at large does not understand the moral arguments for the family, perhaps it will gain some appreciation for the practical arguments. And the recent bad news has been good news in this regard. Our arguments have been given a huge boost with the collapse of the world financial markets and the continuing economic fallout.

An economy built on massive lending and spending cannot be sustained. But the reason it cannot be sustained is not merely economic, it is moral. It regards material wealth as the ultimate goal, and people as merely a commodity to achieve that goal. It is selfish and therefore self-destructive.

An economy based on the family is self-sustaining. Its focus is on the nurturing and training of children and not on the mere acquisition of goods. The family ideal as defended by Chesterton is something quite different than the industrialized consumer family, where the family members leave the house each morning by the clock and on a strict schedule to pursue work and recreation and the majority of life outside the home. Chesterton's ideal was the productive home with its creative kitchen, its busy workshop, its fruitful garden, and its central role in entertainment, education, and livelihood. Unlike the industrial home, life in a productive household is not amenable to scheduling and anything but predictable.

The only thing surprising about this ideal is that it was once shared by almost everyone. Children used to be considered an asset; at some point they began to be seen as a liability.

Chesterton saw the beginning of this problem when he noticed people preferring to buy amusements for themselves rather than to have children. He pointed out prophetically that children are a far better form of entertainment than electrical gadgets. The irony today is that the retailers that sell the electronic amusements are going out of business because there are not enough people to buy this merchandise.

But there is another worse problem why children are now considered a liability. They don't merely make other material desires cost-prohibitive. They are cost-prohibitive themselves. They must be educated. The cost of educating them is obscene. A college education is the most overpriced product on the planet, and over-rated as well. Parents have the privilege of sacrificing nearly everything to send their children to college, only to have them get their heads filled with doubts and destructive ideas, undermining everything their parents have taught them.

But there are fewer parents because there are fewer children.

When social security was instituted, 15 workers supported each retiree. Now each retiree is supported by only three workers.

Those of us who are still working spend 15% of our income to support those who aren't working.

Our lack of domestic life is reflected in the fact that we don't have a domestic economy. We don't produce anything. We are suddenly watching massive layoffs, but the people laid off (no offense to them) were not producing anything. They were either selling things, or sitting at desks and computer terminals, being paid with borrowed money, so that they could also go into debt. Now the financial center of the country has moved from New York to Washington, D.C., as Gudge has passed the baton to Hudge, who has promised that all the problems that were caused by too much borrowing will all be solved by even more borrowing.

The younger generation cannot support the older generation because we have committed demographic suicide. We are paying a high price not only for slaughtering our unborn children but for contracepting them. In fact, we have demonstrated that we cannot afford the high price.

We have seen the natural consequences of unnatural acts. We have witnessed a monumental economic disaster that is not the result of inflation or recession but of the devaluation of children.

Chesterton says that every high civilization decays by forgetting obvious things. The obvious things are the ordinary things, and we have forgotten them. The modern world that we have created has brought with it great strain and stress so that even the things that normal men have normally desired are no longer desirable: "marriage and fair ownership and worship and the mysterious worth of man." Those are the normal and ordinary things. Those are the things we have lost, and we need to recover them.

"The disintegration of rational society," says Chesterton, "started in the drift from the hearth and the family; the solution must be a drift back."

Chapter Eighteen

BY THEIR FRUITS—OR LACK THEREOF—YOU WILL KNOW THEM

The faith and the family go together and must be defended together. An attack on one is usually an attack on the other, and the attacks, though always persistent and sometimes vicious, are not so difficult to defend against after all. It is simply a matter of being reasonable and being as persistent as those who insist on misunderstanding or misrepresenting the faith and the family, even those who are bent on destroying them.

One of the most common criticisms against the Catholic faith is that it is out of step with the modern world. That's not much of a criticism. We pretty much agree with that, only we feel that the problem is not with the faith, but with the modern world. Too often we are reactionary in our response to critics rather than taking the initiative and putting the critics on the spot. We need to become more adept at painting them into a corner where they will find themselves having to defend the mess that is the modern world.

For the last one hundred years there has been an attack on marriage and the family that began with "birth control" (contraception), continued with "choice" and "reproductive health" (abortion and infanticide), and has now arrived at the brashest oxymoron of all: "gay marriage" (the attempted normalization of the most abnormal of human acts—homosexuality). G.K.

Chesterton recommends that we show no respect for the "sentimental rhetoric" that is used by such enemies of the family. We need to point out clearly how obviously unnatural all of these things are, and more importantly, we need to hold up high the Catholic ideal for the family, not only because it is right but because it is the only defensible position.

To the common objection that our ideal of marriage is simply an ideal, that it cannot be a reality, Chesterton's response is: "It is an ideal in a diseased society, it is a reality in a healthy society. For where it is real it makes society healthy." He readily admits that it will not make the society perfectly healthy, because Catholics also believe in other things besides marriage: sin, for instance. But the point is that the Catholic sacrament of marriage is still more reasonable, more sane, more natural, more practical than all its grotesque imitators and outright defilers. It might be more difficult because it requires something unheard of in the modern world: sacrifice. The world only wants what is easiest at the moment.

Chesterton says, "Love is subject to law because it is subject to life." Lifeless love is not love. Though the world exalts lust as love for love's sake, it is ultimately unfulfilling. It is empty. It is barren. It is a desert not a garden. The Church teaches love for *life's* sake. Chesterton says that in marriage, "passion is purified by its own fruitfulness, when that fruitfulness is its dignified and decent end." As a sacrament, it is a fulfillment of Christ's teaching that He, Love Incarnate, has come that we may have life and that we may have it more abundantly. We are called to be fruitful. This is no mere metaphor. It is one of the first commands of God in Genesis. It is reflected in the Gospels, in Christ's words, "By their fruits you shall know them." All the jokes about Catholics and their large families are very recent in origin. Until the early part of the last century, all Christian churches condemned the use of contraceptives. But one-by-one, the Protestant sects caved in to the world's desires. With the rise of contraception came a parallel rise in divorce, which had also once been universally condemned among Christians. Then came abortion. Same thing happened. Only a few Protestant churches openly condemn abortion anymore. Then came the bland acceptance of practicing homosexuals (practicing for what?). One of the Catholic Church's closest cousins, the Episcopal Church, ordained an openly homosexual bishop. Meanwhile the world sneers derisively at the Catholic Church for maintaining its teaching about the sacrament of marriage.

The practical result of Catholic teaching is that we will win the war against the Culture of Death by having babies and raising them to be faithful to the Church. Our poor misguided enemies have a very self-defeating strategy. The world has countered the Church's teaching with the false alarm of overpopulation. But the cold facts indicate that the nations that accept contraception and abortion and homosexuality simply are not replacing themselves. By their fruits you shall know them. By their lack of fruits you won't know them because they won't be there.

Chesterton points out the irony that the modern industrial states that have invoked "a nightmare of over-population" did so after having themselves "actually destroyed the monastic brotherhoods that were a voluntary and virile limitation of it. In other words, they are rather reluctantly relapsing into birth control after actually suppressing the proof that men are capable of self-control." This idea of self-control is another puzzle to the modern world. But celibacy is the accompanying ideal to marriage. And Chesterton calls it "a poetic and positive enthusiasm, where all others would make it merely a negative mutilation."

The Catholic ideal of marriage can save our society. It is the only reasonable alternative to the bizarre anarchy we are facing.

It is the only normal thing. A thing so normal will not disappear, says Chesterton, "amid the accidents of an abnormal society. The society will never be able to judge marriage. Marriage will judge that society; and may possibly condemn it."

Chapter Nineteen

THE MEANING OF BABIES

G.K. Chesterton says that every time a new baby is born, it is as if God has created a new sun and a new moon, because there is a new person to appreciate the sun and moon, a new set of eyes looking at God's light. Everything is remade, "and the universe is put again on its trial."

My wife and I have had this amazing experience of God's re-creation six times.

When announcing the good news of the birth of our sixth child, Gabriel Benedict Ahlquist, I encountered a very typical reaction.

First question: "Is this your first child?"

Answer: "No, sixth."

Second question: "Is this your second wife?"

Answer: "No, first."

The third question is either, "Haven't you figured it out yet?" or "What are you, Catholic or something?"

Answer: "Yes."

Call it an opportunity for evangelization.

Note the sequence of questions and the assumptions behind them: First child? Second wife? Are you (1.) stupid? or (2.) Catholic?

There was a time when having babies was considered a normal thing, when having brothers and sisters was considered a normal thing because the mother and father were normal parents, when there was a normal and healthy attitude towards sex. If you go back far enough, there was even a time when being Catholic was normal. But people are now scandalized by the idea of anyone using sex for the purpose of pro-creation, especially married people, and of anyone taking their own religion seriously. The rule has become the exception. The world has things exactly backwards.

The greatest event of life—birth—is regarded as trivial, a nuisance, even some kind of curse. The most disposable things in the world—clothes, cars, computers—are regarded as essential. The acquisition of these secondary things is obviously put in jeopardy by the arrival of that primary thing called a child. Our first reaction is generally selfish: this is going to cramp my style, and how am I going to afford this? But a child is something more than a mere diversion and something that cannot be calculated as a mere expense. It is not only the universe that is put to the test, it is *you*. You must teach this new soul, and will be surprised to find out that this new person will also teach you. You will nurture this soul, and it will nurture you. It will happen because you will be devoted to this person just as your parents were devoted to you; a splendid tradition that goes back, I'm told, a very long ways.

The Holy Family is the model family because every father must be St. Joseph, the craftsman, the provider, the protector, the guide. Every mother must be Mary: humble, dutiful, glorious, merciful. And every child must be regarded as God come down to earth, a divine presence, a miracle.

Chesterton explains this devotional role of parents:

> You and I would certainly not be the splendid public monuments that we are if our fathers and mothers had not given us not only a great deal more devotion than we deserved, but a great deal more devotion than we in any strictly ascertainable

and scientific sense required. But that immoderate consideration was necessary to produce even moderate results; the infant has to be treated as much better than he is so that in the long run he may be not quite so bad as he might have been. The child has to begin as a god, in the faint hope that he may end as a man.

When we consider even for a moment the profound experience of parenting, it makes perfect sense why people who have prevented themselves from becoming parents, who have chosen the secondary things over the primary things, are not happy with their decision. They are restless. They seek excitement elsewhere. They are never at home. After all, there is no one there. We could even say there is no home there.

Our society has thrown out the baby with the bathwater, or, rather thrown out the baby and kept the bathwater. We see it in the clean and unlived-in look of our suburban homes that have more bathrooms than bedrooms. It all looks very sterile. It is.

Chesterton says that anyone "who cannot see that a baby is marvelous could not see that anything was marvelous." Yet, they are the ones making the hilarious wisecracks about Catholics having babies. I'm always ready to laugh, but reluctant when the joke is on them.

I was also told—seriously—that Catholics are trying to take over the world by having so many children. Well, I never thought of that. I suppose it is a rather easy way to take over the world compared with other schemes. Strange, though, that our opponents see such a good strategy but refuse to use it. Instead they actively reduce their own numbers. It is an ineffectual way to fight. But I must say, I would rather win the world by conversion, not by our opponents merely destroying themselves through the Culture of Death.

Chesterton points out that the Church has been "ludicrously accused of being gloomy and the enemy of life," and yet it has "distinguished itself among the creeds of the world by its quite peculiar insistence on the fact that life is sacred."

Chapter Twenty

LOOKING FOR LOVE IN ALL
THE WRONG PLACES

I am often asked for the source of the quotation, "A man knock-ing on the door of a brothel is knocking for God." The line has been attributed to G.K. Chesterton because it is startling and obviously paradoxical. It tells a truth that is the opposite of what we expect. We assume that a man consciously sinning is avoiding God. And though this is true, there is a more profound truth that a man seeking a thrill, seeking comfort, seeking pleasure, is really yearning for something more than the shallow and disappointing experience he is going to find in soulless sex.

The quotation, as it turns out, is not from Chesterton. It is from a Scottish writer named Bruce Marshall, a Catholic convert, who was a soldier in World War I where he lost a leg. In 1945, he wrote a bestselling book called *The World, The Flesh, and Father Smith*. It is a sweet and reflective story, filled with quiet integrity, and well worth reading. The famous line actually reads: "I still prefer to believe that sex is a substitute for religion and that the young man who rings the bell at the brothel is unconsciously looking for God."

There are two kinds of sexual sin. One is the kind designed for immediate regret, the epitome of what St. Paul talks about in Romans, Chapter 7, when he bemoans doing the very thing he hates and wonders who will deliver him. In the very next breath he praises God that deliverance comes through Jesus Christ. Likewise, in Psalm 51, the great Psalm of Repentance, David is regretting his adulterous affair with Bathsheba. The opening words of the Psalm are the opening prayer at every Mass: "Lord, have mercy." The Psalm goes on to invoke God to "Wash me, and I will be whiter than snow," to "Restore to me the joy of your salvation," and to "Create in me a pure heart." There can be no better prayers than these. It is a repentance that leads to evangelization: "Then I will teach transgressors your ways, and sinners will return to you."

But there is another kind of sexual sin, the kind that is not regretted but rationalized, not repented but repeated. These are not sins followed by prayer, but carried on with the attitude of telling God what to do. They are no longer merely sins of the flesh. They are sins of the soul.

Chesterton makes the distinction between to the two kinds of sin: he says the sins of men are wine and wenching, but the sins of devils are rebellion and spiritual pride. Pride is the supreme evil. Pride can make a vice out of any virtue. The Proverbs say that pride goes before a fall, but as Chesterton says, pride *is* a fall. It is pride that truly separates us from God because it keeps us from getting on our knees and confessing our sins. It is most telling that the sexual sin with the highest currency these days is not only not regretted but celebrated, not mourned but called "gay," and even defiantly accompanied by the word "pride."

It is also interesting to see who understands the importance of humility and who does not. In *The World, The Flesh, and Father Smith*, Bruce Marshall observes that the Catholic Church has always been full of people who are either educated or uneducated, but "it is the half-educated who have always been too proud to come in." You can find a pure heart in those who know almost nothing of the faith ("the poor in spirit") and in those who know almost everything (Job, who puts his hand over his mouth). But those who have grasped only a few things, with an air of sufficiency and self-satisfaction, who have exalted their partial truths against the whole truth, they have not come clean with God.

What about that man knocking at the brothel door: is he the humble sinner or the proud sinner? It is perhaps easier to make the case that it is the humble sinner who is looking for God. But I think we could argue that even the proud sinner is looking for God. He is the one, who, as Bruce Marshall says, is using sex as a substitute for religion. It is true that he is unwilling to let go of his selfish desires, not willing to trust himself to something less immediate, less tangible, but ultimately more profound and more fulfilling. He knows he is accepting a false thing in place of the real thing. But the real thing is what he really wants. He will never be satisfied with anything less. He is simply looking for love in all the wrong places.

Chapter Twenty-One

NOT GAY AND NOT MARRIAGE

One of the pressing issues of Chesterton's time was "birth control." He not only objected to the idea, he objected to the very term because it meant the opposite of what it said. It meant no birth and no control. I can only imagine he would have the same objections about "gay marriage." The idea is wrong, but so is the name. It is not gay and it is not marriage.

Chesterton is so consistently right in his pronouncements and prophecies because he understands that anything that attacks the family is bad for society. That is why he speaks out against Eugenics and contraception, against divorce and "free love" (another term he dislikes because of its dishonesty), but also against wage slavery and compulsory state-sponsored education and mothers hiring other people to do what mothers are designed to do themselves. It is safe to say that Chesterton stands up against every trend and fad that plague us today because every one of those trends and fads undermines the family. Big Government tries to replace the family's authority, and Big Business tries to replace the family's autonomy. There is a constant commercial and cultural pressure on father, mother, and child. They are minimized and marginalized and, yes, mocked. But as Chesterton says, "This triangle of truisms, of father, mother and child, cannot be destroyed; it can only destroy those civilizations which disregard it."

This latest attack on the family is neither the latest nor the worst. But it has a shock value to it, in spite of the process of de-sensitization that the information and entertainment industries have been putting us through the past several years. Those who have tried to speak out against the normalization of the abnormal have been met with "either slanging or silence," as Chesterton was when he attempted to argue against the faddish philosophies that were promoted by the major newspapers in his day. In 1926, he warned, "The next great heresy will be an attack on morality, especially sexual morality." His warning has gone unheeded, and sexual morality has decayed progressively. But let us remember that it began with birth control, which is an attempt to create sex for sex's sake, changing the act of love into an act of selfishness. The promotion and acceptance of lifeless, barren, selfish sex has logically progressed to homosexuality.

Chesterton shows that the problem of homosexuality as an enemy of civilization is quite old. In *The Everlasting Man*, he describes the nature-worship and "mere mythology" that produced a perversion among the Greeks. "Just as they became unnatural by worshipping nature, so they actually became unmanly by worshipping man." Any young man, he says, "who has the luck to grow up sane and simple" is naturally repulsed by homosexuality because "it is not true to human nature or to common sense." He argues that if we attempt to act indifferent about it, we are fooling ourselves. It is "the illusion of familiarity," when a perversion becomes a convention.

In his book *Heretics*, Chesterton seems to prophesy of the misuse of the word "gay." He writes of "the very powerful and very desolate philosophy of Oscar Wilde. It is the *carpe diem* religion." *Carpe diem* means "seize the day," do whatever you want and don't think about the consequences, live only for the moment. "But the *carpe diem* religion is not the religion of happy people, but of very unhappy people." There is a hopelessness as well as a haplessness to it. When sex is only a momentary pleasure, when it offers nothing beyond itself, it brings no fulfillment. It is literally lifeless. And as Chesterton writes in his book *St. Francis of Assisi,* the minute sex ceases to be a servant, it becomes a master. This is perhaps the most profound analysis of the problem of homosexuals: they are slaves to sex. They are trying to "pervert the future and unmake the past." They need to be set free.

Sin has consequences. Yet Chesterton always maintains that we must condemn the sin and not the sinner. And no one shows more compassion for the fallen than G.K. Chesterton. Of Oscar Wilde, whom he calls "the Chief of the Decadents," he says that Wilde committed "a monstrous wrong" but also suffered monstrously for it, going to an awful prison, where he was forgotten by all the people who had earlier toasted his cavalier rebelliousness. "His was a complete life, in that awful sense in which your life and mine are incomplete; since we have not yet paid for our sins. In that sense one might call it a perfect life, as one speaks of a perfect equation; it cancels out. On the one hand we have the healthy horror of the evil; on the other the healthy horror of the punishment."

Chesterton referred to Wilde's homosexual behavior as a "highly civilized" sin, something that was a worse affliction among the wealthy and cultured classes. It was a sin that was never a temptation for Chesterton, but he says that it is no great virtue for us never to commit a sin for which we are not tempted. That is another reason we must treat our homosexual brothers and sisters with compassion. We know our own sins and weaknesses well enough. There is a great proverb attributed to Philo of Alexandria: "Be kind. Everyone you meet is fighting a terrible battle." But compassion must never compromise with evil. Chesterton reminds us of to keep our balance, that our truth must not be pitiless, but neither can our pity be untruthful. Homosexuality *is* a disorder. It is contrary to order. Homosexual acts are sinful, that is, they are contrary to God's order. They can never be normal. And worse yet, they can never even be even. As Chesterton's great detective Father Brown says: "Men may keep a sort of level of good, but no man has ever been able to keep on one level of evil. That road goes down and down."

Marriage is between a man and a woman. That is the created order of things. And the Catholic Church teaches that it is a sacramental order, with divine implications. The world has made a mockery of marriage that has now culminated with homosexual unions. But it was heterosexual men and women who paved the way to this decay. Divorce, which is an abnormal thing, is now treated as normal. Contraception, another abnormal thing, is now treated as normal. Abortion is still not normal, but it is legal. Making homosexual "marriage" legal will not make it normal, but it will add to the confusion of the times. And it will add to the downward spiral of our civilization. But Chesterton's prophecy remains potent and portent: We will not be able to destroy the family. We will merely destroy ourselves by disregarding the family.

ஃ

Chapter Twenty-Two

AN ARGUMENT IN DEFENSE
OF MARRIAGE THAT YOU'VE
NEVER THOUGHT OF

G.K. Chesterton says that he has known many happy marriages, but never a *peaceful* one. "The fairy tales said that the prince and princess lived happily ever afterwards: and so they did. They lived happily, although it is very likely that from time to time they threw the furniture at each other. Most marriages, I think, are happy marriages; but there is no such thing as a contented marriage. The whole pleasure of marriage is that it is a perpetual crisis."

He also says he has known many happy marriages, but never a *compatible* one. "If Americans can be divorced for 'incompatibility' I cannot conceive why they are not all divorced... The whole aim of marriage is to fight through and survive the instant when incompatibility becomes unquestionable. For a man and a woman, as such, are incompatible."

So, here is an argument in defense of marriage that you had not thought of. The reason why marriage must be between a man and a woman is that men and women are incompatible.

Everything about a same-sex "marriage" is against natural law, but few people will sit still long enough for the natural law argument to be laid out for them. And it is not because they are impatient. It is because they see immediately where that

Chapter Twenty-Two

AN ARGUMENT IN DEFENSE OF MARRIAGE THAT YOU'VE NEVER THOUGHT OF

G.K. Chesterton says that he has known many happy marriages, but never a *peaceful* one. "The fairy tales said that the prince and princess lived happily ever afterwards: and so they did. They lived happily, although it is very likely that from time to time they threw the furniture at each other. Most marriages, I think, are happy marriages; but there is no such thing as a contented marriage. The whole pleasure of marriage is that it is a perpetual crisis."

He also says he has known many happy marriages, but never a *compatible* one. "If Americans can be divorced for 'incompatibility' I cannot conceive why they are not all divorced... The whole aim of marriage is to fight through and survive the instant when incompatibility becomes unquestionable. For a man and a woman, as such, are incompatible."

So, here is an argument in defense of marriage that you had not thought of. The reason why marriage must be between a man and a woman is that men and women are incompatible.

Everything about a same-sex "marriage" is against natural law, but few people will sit still long enough for the natural law argument to be laid out for them. And it is not because they are impatient. It is because they see immediately where that

105

argument is going, and they do not want wait for the obvious conclusion. They understand pretty quickly the connection between sex and children. Sex and procreation are natural. Contraception is unnatural. It is unnatural either when a man and woman are trying to avoid the natural consequences of sex, or when two members of the same gender are trying to avoid the natural *act* of sex. People do not want to think that contraception and homosexuality are part of the same perversion against nature. They don't want to think about it, and yet those who favor widespread contraception also favor same-sex "marriage." Both attack the fundamental nature of marriage. But as I say, no one sits still long enough for this argument.

But an argument that might get their attention is the incompatibility argument. It has a shocking quality to it, and even today people are sometimes invigorated by a good jolt. It is shocking to say that men and women are not only different, but that marriage demands that difference: not just the biological differences needed for two people to become a father and a mother, but the differences beyond biology needed for them to become a husband and wife.

These supra-biological differences are not slight, and they are not imaginary. In fact, Chesterton says:

> The differences between a man and a woman are at best so obstinate and exasperating that they practically cannot be got over unless there is an atmosphere of exaggerated tenderness and mutual interest. To put the matter in one metaphor, the sexes are two stubborn pieces of iron; if they are to be welded together, it must be while they are red-hot. Every woman has to find out that the husband is a selfish beast, because every man is a selfish beast by the standard of a woman. But let

her find out the beast while they are both still in the story of 'Beauty and the Beast.' Every man has to find out that is his wife is cross—that is to say, sensitive to the point of madness; for every woman is mad by the masculine standard. But let him find out that she is mad while her madness is more worth considering than anyone else's sanity."

A few years ago there was pop-psychology book that came along arguing that men and women are from two different planets, men from Mars and women from Venus. That does not go nearly far enough but at least it approaches the right idea, and it hit the bestseller lists because it hit on an obvious truth that people were drawn to hear. The right idea can be stated very simply: men are men, and women are women. They are not the same. They look at the world differently, at each other differently, at themselves differently. Thus, a father is not a mother, and a mother is not a father. A child needs both of those perspectives to see wholly and clearly, just as he needs both of his eyes to see clearly.

The attack on gender has tried to do away with these differences between men and women, with boys being discouraged from being boys and girls from being girls. We have seen the subsequent occurrences of feminine men and masculine women, but nobody is fooled by the bizarre results. Their very oddity only affirms what is normal.

But, as Chesterton maintains, they are not just different: they are incompatible. "Marriage," he says, "is a duel to the death." It is precisely the tension between a man and a woman, a husband and a wife, that makes marriage so interesting and beautiful, like the tension on a violin string.

"The bridge built between the two sexes," he says, is the greatest feat of engineering in all of history. Which is to say that same-sex "marriage" is a bridge that doesn't go anywhere. It stays on the same side of the river.

This latest attack on marriage is only the latest. It is not the last. It may damage that bridge built between man and woman, that bridge known as marriage, but it will not destroy it. Chesterton says that marriage is attacked "not because it is a vanishing institution, but because it is an enduring institution. People jeer at it because they will not change it. People batter it because it will not fall."

One of the reasons that it will not fall is the balance provided by the two incompatible characters on each end.

The best thing about this argument is that none of the arguments against it are any good at all.

ॐ

Chapter Twenty-Three

A SURPRISING CAUSE OF CONFUSION

I once had the misfortune to watch a television program about the economic crisis. There was some attempt being made to explain why people kept investing in schemes that really were not very sound, why they kept getting bigger mortgages than they could afford to pay back, why they kept believing that the value of real estate would keep increasing forever, why they kept trying to increase their wealth by plunging into unsustainable debt, and so on. It was an almost useful analysis until there suddenly appeared on the screen some psychologist from some big university who had been doing some major research. He had conducted a bunch of brain scans of the "oldest" part of the brain. Not sure what that means. He talked about "that part of the brain that we share with most other animals, even lizards." Still not sure what that means. The psychologist explained that this was the part of the brain that is most stimulated by sex, drugs, and food. And his big discovery is that it is also stimulated by money. This then is the source of powerful "irrational" emotions.

I did not know that lizards are stimulated by money. I suspect rather that the psychologists are stimulated by grant money. But in any case, I think the real explanation of people's bad behavior regarding money might be found in a good theology department where they still talk about sin. However, such theology departments are difficult to find, and likely do not pull in much grant money. Nobody wants to fund research into sin. At least, not if it is called sin.   Certainly not if it is called by the specific sin of greed.

We never hear about sin. Unless of course, a Catholic, especially a Catholic priest, is found guilty of a sin. Then we hear all about it. The world does not wish to apply any moral standards to the world, only to the Church.

The world ridicules innocence, but it also ridicules guilt. G.K. Chesterton talks about the way the world will mock an innocent girl, who is "always covered with blushes and confusion." But he points out that it is another sort of girl who has "more of the confusion" and "less of the blushes." He goes on to list "confusion of thought, confusion of phraseology, confusion of philosophy."

The confusion of philosophy comes from the denial of sin. The confusion of thought is evident in the way innocence is assumed though not defined. People sneer when it is honored, yet they are outraged when it is defiled. The confusion of phraseology is seen in the way the world casts about trying to avoid the word sin. Sin is explained away with contradictory terms like "sophistication," "emotion," and "irrationality." As a result what we hear from the newspapers and magazines and television and the Internet is something Chesterton describes as "a hash of half a hundred inconsistent philosophies." The denial of sin ranges from naïve ideas about the horrible things people are really capable of, to the rather nonchalant acceptance of whatever it is that people want to do.

Chesterton observes: "The follower of Rousseau tended too much to say: 'I am born in a state of innocence, and therefore I can be as guilty as I like.' But the new skeptics, who also deny Original Sin, seem rather to be saying: 'There is no Original Sin, because everybody can be born bad and behaves as badly as possible without it.' The modern humanitarian believes in Total Depravity without any Fall to explain it."

Without a philosophy of the Fall, it is also difficult to discuss purity. Chesterton points out the same confusion of thought that on the one hand will brashly claim "To the pure in heart all things are pure"; and on the other hand try to explain that there really is no such thing as purity. The same confusion is seen when we all disapprove of prostitution, but do not all approve of purity. But, as Chesterton points out, we cannot deal with a social evil unless we "get at once to the social ideal."

It should not be that difficult to understand what purity is, and that when we talk about purity, we mean something that has not been befouled by something that befouls, namely sin. There is something all-or-nothing about purity. Purity needs to be completely pure to get itself so called. A little purity does not go very far. A teaspoon of clean water does not purify a tall glass of sewage, but a teaspoon of sewage utterly ruins a glass of clean water. But physical cleanliness should not be confused with moral purity. As Chesterton says, "Saints can afford to be dirty, but seducers have to be clean."

Chastity is sexual purity. Virginity was an ideal even in the pagan world, but it was Christianity that actually found a way to live out the ideal. Though the modern world seems utterly mystified by the ideal, Chesterton points out that there is an unconscious acknowledgement of it in the modern worship of children. Why else, he asks, would anyone "worship a thing merely because it is small and immature?" It is because we value purity.

But there is still such a thing as chaste sex. It is within the blessed bond of marriage. Something else the world does not understand: that sex should be restricted to a man and woman who are married to each other and open to the life-giving act.

The world does not understand it because of the aforementioned confusion. In stunning contrast, says Chesterton, "The reward of chastity is a clearness of the intellect."

Chapter Twenty-Four

THE OTHER GOD

Through no fault of my own, I once had to attend a seminar on financial planning. The first requirement, it would seem, for financial planning is that you have some finances with which to plan. Since I failed to meet this requirement in a spectacular fashion, it made no sense that I was there. But there I was. And I must say that I learned a lot. For instance:

ò▲ Insurance is really a form of gambling. Not to buy insurance is also a form a gambling. You simply have to decide which is the better bet. As with all gambling, the odds are against you. You will lose.

ò▲ There is no disability insurance for "full-time homemakers." You must have a "job" to be able to get disability insurance. A "job" is something you get paid to do.

ò▲ Divorce messes up financial planning. In order to retain your wealth, you must protect it from your spouse with a pre-nuptial agreement.

ò▲ Children mess up financial planning. In order to build and maintain wealth, you should not have children. Children make money disappear. Especially if you decide you want the children to be educated.

🦋 Illness messes up financial planning. Don't get sick.

🦋 Death messes up financial planning. Don't die.

I should point out that the instructor did not actually say these things. But anyone taking notes would have inferred them, as I did. He actually did say that when he explains how much college costs, it usually serves as an effective means of birth control. Which, of course, would be funny if it were not so sad.

He also said that financial planning has nothing to do with love. Well, yes it does. It has to do with love of money. Plan right and you will be plenty rich. Your only problem then will be what to do with all the money. Never mind that most people with a lot of money have found that money does not make them happy. They are in a sense homeless because they own too many homes. They acquire endless possessions to fill an empty hole in their souls. They travel as a way of running away. They get pets, wishing they had children. They treat dogs like babies. Their world in fact shrinks. They become prisoners of their money.

One of the most consistent but overlooked themes in the Bible is the spiritual peril caused by wealth.

It starts with the Ten Commandments, all of which, of course, get neglected in our society. But the Tenth Commandment, that one about not coveting our neighbor's goods, is completely trampled on in our commercial culture, which is built on covetousness.

Ecclesiastes says, "He who loves money will not be satisfied with money." And also: "Sweet is the sleep of the laborer, whether he has eaten little or much. But the surfeit of the rich will not let him sleep." (Guilt as well as overeating also keeps people awake, but I understand there are drugs to deal with this.)

The prophet Amos rails against the materialism and love of luxury of his age that have caused the privileged classes to forget both God and their fellow man. Seems like he was writing about 2700 years ahead of his time.

In the Gospels, Jesus says plainly that we cannot worship both God and Mammon. We can only serve one or the other. Mammon is money with a capital M. And more than one parable points to what happens to the man with misplaced priorities: "What does it profit a man if he should gain the whole world and lose his soul?"

And in the Epistles, St. Paul warns that the love of money is the root of all evil.

We live in a society that openly worships Mammon instead of God, that stands in awe before great wealth, that has sacrificed its children to Mammon, and that unashamedly teaches us how to protect our money from our family.

As I sat in that classroom being taught that love has nothing to do with financial planning, it occurred to me that the truth is exactly the other way around. Planning for the future means counting on love, which is why a husband and wife make a vow to each other that they are expected to be able to count on and why the Church strengthens this vow with a sacrament. Pre-nuptial agreements have nothing to do with love. Love is unselfish. Money is all about selfishness. It breeds greed. It does not breed children.

Love creates. Love creates children. Love gives everything. It gives everything to the family. Proper financial planning has everything to do with love. You invest in your children. And your children are your insurance.

If we are honest, if we work hard, if we pray "Give us this day our daily bread," it is amazing how God will keep his promises and take care of us.

The proper attitude toward money is that we should be stewards: responsible, not reckless, but also not selfish. Thrift means living within our means, but it also means to thrive. Thriving does not mean having a lot of money. It means living life to its fullest by appreciating all the good things that God has already given us.

Stewardship also means giving back to God a portion of what he has given to us. It means being unfailingly generous both to the Church and to the poor.

As for wealth, as for any excess money that falls to us that goes far beyond our needs, the teaching of the Church and the Gospels could not be more clear: "To whom much is given, much will be required." Or, as Chesterton says, "The purpose of wealth is to chuck it."

If I had taught the class on financial planning, it would have been over in about five minutes.

Chapter Twenty-Five

ANOTHER SIN YOU DON'T WANT TO HEAR ABOUT
(In fact, if I tell you what it is, you won't read this chapter)

The Church is always condemned for condemning sins. Since we are all sinners, sin is the last thing we want to hear about. But of course, if we do not confess our sins and flee from our sins, sin is the last thing we WILL hear about. Last, as in Last Judgment. That is why the Church has a certain obligation to keep bringing these things up.

The Church has to do the hard and thankless work of condemning sins. There are few folks—well, more than a few—who do not consider the Church a trustworthy authority on the subject of sin. They are quick to point out that priests and bishops and even popes have turned out to be guilty of the same sins they have condemned. But this excuse for questioning the authority of the Church does not wear well. It is hypocritical to criticize hypocrites. The more interesting challenge is this: do sins change? Or rather: does the Catholic Church condemn something as being a sin in one age, but excuse it as not being a sin in another age? This is an argument that is often used against the Church's moral teaching.

In the 1960s many people in the Catholic Church were anticipating that Pope Paul VI was going to issue an encyclical that would permit contraception. Some argued that there was precedent for such a change in the Church's teaching. After all, the Church once condemned usury as a sin, but no longer did.

But the encyclical *Humane Vitae* surprised and infuriated a lot of people: the Pope upheld the Church's teachings instead of altering them. He also warned about what would happen if the world embraced a contraceptive mentality: it would lead to abortion, divorce, and sexual perversion. Turned out he was right.

But in the social and religious chaos of the second half of the 20th century, most everyone missed an important point that is now coming to bear on the economic chaos of the early 21st century: the Church also never changed its teaching on usury. Like contraception, usury is still a sin.

It was condemned right from the beginning. In Psalm 15 we hear: "Lord, who may abide in your tent? Who may dwell on your holy mountain? Whoever walks without blame, doing what is right, speaking truth from the heart…who keeps an oath despite the cost, lends no money at interest…" Take a look also at Exodus 22:24, Leviticus 25:36-27, Deuteronomy 23:20—all of which clearly forbid usury.

Usury was also condemned by the classical pagan philosophers, Plato and Aristotle.

The theme was taken up by St. Jerome, St. Ambrose, St. Augustine, and other Church Fathers, who attacked usury in no uncertain terms. Several popes, including St. Leo the Great, Gregory IX and Innocent III spoke out against usury. In the 14th century, Pope Benedict XIV issued an encyclical specifically upholding the condemnation against usury, saying the Church had not changed its position (just as Pope Paul VI made clear with regards to contraception). At least five Church Councils condemned usury, including the famous Nicene Council, which gave us our Creed, and the Second Lateran Council, which called usury "despicable and blameworthy by divine and human laws."

The great Doctor of the Church, St. Thomas Aquinas, makes it clear: "To take usury for money lent is unjust in itself, because this is to sell what does not exist, and this…leads to inequality which is contrary to justice." He argues that economic exchange is necessary to maintain a society, but unjust exchange will destroy a society, and usury, as he points out, is an example of unjust exchange.

Even Chaucer wrote that usury is "hateful to Christ and to His company."

The Church did not change its position against usury. The problem is the world changed its position. Chesterton points out that during the High Middle Ages, or what he calls "the highpoint of Christian society," usury was "everywhere denounced and forbidden." But now it is "everywhere flattered and condoned." What was condemned by all of Western civilization for centuries during the time it was led by the Church, was suddenly embraced by that civilization in the wake of the Reformation and the Enlightenment—and the rejection of faith and reason. As we have grown "much vaguer about usury being usury," we have grown much vaguer about all the other sins being sinful.

And what do we have to show for our ignoring this teaching of the Church? As of this writing, $11.68 trillion in consumer debt. $854.2 billion in credit card debt. Over 20% of home mortgages that exceed the value of the property. A government that keeps spending money that it does not have. A borrowing mentality that never considers how it is going to pay anything back. Economic collapse. Echoing the Popes and the Saints before him, Chesterton warns that usury devours and destroys: "It is a gigantic heap of debt, like a heap of dirt. It is a heap of debts hoarded until they have gone bad. It is now a heap of bad debts which a little more bad debt will send toppling into the mire."

Interestingly enough, there is a connection between contraception and usury. Both are a form of taking the pleasure without paying for it, of being irresponsible and selfish, rather than productive and charitable. "Usury," says Chesterton, "is in its nature at war with life."

But just as most people do not want to hear about the sin of contraception, most people do not want to hear about the sin of usury, because most people do not want to hear about sin. That continues to be a problem. Prophets like Chesterton remind us about these things, and we react as most people have reacted to prophets: We do not listen. "Though men may grow used to usury, and even practise it without shame under the present professional standard, yet God does not grow used to usury, any more than to murder or to devil-worship..." Strong words.

And to anyone who would make the argument that our economy and our society depends on ignoring this Church teaching, Chesterton offers an equally stern rebuke: "It is a lie to say that the monstrous complicated accumulation of modern finance is essential to civilization, or the social and moral well-being of ordinary men and women."

How do we get out of the mess we are in? There is only one escape from sin. Forgiveness. Let us start by praying the Our Father, and considering the literal meaning of "Forgive us our trespasses...", which is: "Forgive us our debts as we forgive our debtors."

Chapter Twenty-Six

THE POPE'S MESSAGE TO AMERICA

America is unique. As G.K. Chesterton said, it is the only nation ever founded on a creed. That creed is the belief in the right to Life, Liberty, and the Pursuit of Happiness. As most of us know, each of those things is now under attack: the right to Life has been denied to the most vulnerable; the right to Liberty has been strangled unwittingly by governmental girth and political correctness; and the Pursuit of Happiness has been twisted by the culture-at-large into the Pursuit of Unhappiness in the phantom shapes of money, sex, and power.

But our American Creed is still a powerful thing. Liberty is our uniquely American obsession. We talk about it, praise it, appreciate it more than anyone. It draws the rest of the world to us. It is certainly our greatest strength; it is also, unfortunately, our greatest weakness. What is the proper Catholic perspective of Liberty, American Style?

About thirty years after the conclusion of the Vatican Council, the Pope wrote a letter to the American Bishops. It is amazing how many Catholics have forgotten it, or never even know what he said. It would be a good idea to be reminded of his message to America.

Catholics of every nation of course add their own distinctiveness to the Universal Church. In his letter, the Pope says the Church has "never disregarded the manners and customs of the various nations it embraces," and has always been willing to modify the rule of life in a particular environment if it is "required for the salvation of souls." However, while he justly praises the unique accomplishments of American Catholicism, he adds that the Church can never compromise its central doctrine and discipline. He observes that America is quite hostile to Catholic doctrine and discipline. Unfortunately, that hostility does not only come from non-Catholics. There are some American Catholics who are more American than they are Catholic. They are "followers of novelties" who wish that "a certain liberty" would be introduced into the Church. They want the Church to limit "the exercise and vigilance of its powers, so that each of the faithful may act more freely in the pursuit of his natural bent and capacity." In other words, they are infected with chronic American individualism—each person operating according to his own code. Sinatra-itis. I'll do it *My Way*.

The Pope explains that Americans have a common confusion about the meaning of liberty. We think it is the same thing as license: the idea that we can simply do anything we want, say anything we want, print anything we want, defy anything we want. That is not liberty. Liberty means doing the right thing for the right reason. Because we want to do it. Because we know it's the right thing to do. As Chesterton says, to have a right to do a thing does not mean it is right to do it.

America is easily seduced by whatever is new, and American Catholics tend to want to bring these new things into the Church. The Church has never been afraid of new things, and as the Pope makes perfectly clear, the new things have their uses and should be able to thrive "without setting aside the authority and wisdom of the Church," a wisdom and authority grounded in tradition.

But some new things are simply flat wrong. The Pope is aware of that particular American weakness for private revelation and personal interpretations that has given rise to all the various American sects from Mormonism to Seventh Day Adventism to Christian Science. Even among mainline Protestant denominations in America, there is the tendency to think that Americans are some kind of Chosen People, that they have somehow received a greater outpouring of the Holy Spirit. The Pope cautions against such thinking, and reminds us that the spiritual life of the modern world really does not compare with the age of the Apostles and the "valiant martyrs" of the early Church. The evidence suggests that they were led much more powerfully by the Spirit, but the key is that they always operated according to the external guidance of the Church, which America sometimes thinks it no longer needs.

As for new things, the new thing that is always new is the Good News, the Gospel. The Pope emphasizes the importance of evangelism. He says the main reason that people have not become Catholic or dislike Catholics or even differ from Catholics is simply because of ignorance of true Catholic teaching. He urges us to put the truth before everyone "in a familiar and friendly manner." The key to liberty is truth, for as Jesus said, the Truth sets us free.

Perhaps the most important message in the Pope's letter is that obedience to the Church and faithfulness to doctrine are the best way to bring love and justice to the world. Good and faithful American Catholics are not only good for the Church, they are also good for America.

Many American Catholics thought the Vatican Council changed things. The Pope's letter tries to address this misconception. He affirms the great traditions and truths of the Church. He warns against those who think they can depart from this truth, who think that everything "is thrown open to individuals." He affirms that the teaching of the Church is infallible. It is true that he does invoke the "spirit" of the Vatican Council, but he says the purpose of being "guided by its spirit" is so that we might be "preserved from any private error."

As I say, we need to be reminded of his message to America.

The Pope, by the way, was Leo XIII. The Vatican Council he is referring to is the *first* Vatican Council, which concluded in 1870. His letter to the American Bishops was written in 1899.

Chapter Twenty-Seven

MODERNISM AND FUZZY THINKING

The problem with being a prophet is that when you are proved right, it means that the world has gone wrong. One hundred years ago, two prophetic thinkers warned about the same problem at the same time. The problem was Modernism. The prophets were Pope St. Pius X and G.K. Chesterton. The Pope condemned Modernism as the heresy that includes all other heresies. He saw that centuries of the splintering of truth would wreak havoc on the world. Chesterton, too, recognized the chaos of modern ideas undermining all of the great achievements of Western Culture.

Modernism is an obsession with the new and a rebellion against tradition. The Modern world, intoxicated with Darwinism, has been caught up in the cult of endless, mindless Progress, the idea that what is new must naturally be better than what is old. Instead of knowledge being an accumulation of the past, it suddenly became a rejection of the past.

Chesterton defends tradition as being the "Democracy of the Dead." It means giving a vote to our ancestors. Common sense comes from those who came before us. And common sense clearly condemned all the strange ideas that came with Modernism. Not surprisingly, one of the things most categorically condemned by Modernism was common sense. The new-fangled and fashionable ideas came from the elite, the snobs, and the detached intellectuals who were remote from the things that matter most: faith, family, friendship, farms, fortitude.

But the warnings issued by Pope St. Pius X and G.K. Chesterton went unheeded and the result is the mess we see all around us.

The Pope knew that Modernism was an attack on the Church, but that it was also an attack on the world. Chesterton understood this, too. He says that the secularists have not succeeded in destroying religious things, but they have succeeded in destroying secular things. Modernism is certainly recognizable by its destructiveness, but even more so by its self-destructiveness. We see it in contraception, abortion and infanticide. We see it in euthanasia. We see it in teen suicide (which is the result of young people being fed a steady diet of empty ideas and modern despair). We see it in commercialism and consumption and waste, the throwaway mentality. We can also see it in the loss of appreciation for good and beautiful things and in the morbid fascination with the ugly, the bizarre, and the perverse.

Not long ago, the Minneapolis Institute of Arts decided to sell one of its most popular and most lovely paintings: *Bohemienne* ("The Little Gypsy Girl") by William Adolphe Bouguereau, a late-19th century artist who represents the apex of romantic realism. The exquisite painting was of a dark-eyed, black-haired, barefoot girl holding a violin. The Cathedral of Notre Dame rises into the Parisian skies behind her. Her tattered shawl, her translucent skin, her interlocked fingers are not just charming; they are transfixing. She is alive. Her gaze is full of the eternal present, a gaze returned by anyone who has ever looked at the painting. You could stand and stare at it forever.

It was an absolutely stupefying act that the Institute of Arts would even consider selling such a beauty. The museum not only gave a pathetic explanation in defending this decision, it ignored the protests of those who tried to stop the sale of the painting. A donor was even willing to make a large donation to the Museum to *keep* the painting. Nothing like this had ever happened before in the history of the Minneapolis Institute of Arts. But it did no good. The Museum sold the masterpiece at auction. Instead of belonging to the public, it now belongs to a private collector, and may possibly never be displayed in public again.

How could this happen? It happened because the art world reflects the state of the rest of the world. The attack on the exquisite detail of Bouguereau's paintings represents the attack on clarity and definition in ideas as well as in form. The voice of the people, the voice of tradition, is silenced by snobs who prefer the downfall of art to the highpoint of art. They presume to tell us what we should like rather than letting us decide for ourselves. They have dismissed our opinion entirely, which is the voice of common sense. They listen rather to the shrill small voice of the expert.

It all goes back to the heresy of Modernism and the hatred of the traditional and the beautiful. It happened in the Church. It happened in the world. In art, it began harmlessly enough with the blurring of the lines that led to Impressionism. But it quickly degenerated into Cubism and splattered canvasses and utter formlessness. In the family, it began with the blurring of the lines between the sexes that led to ill-defined roles in the family. It quickly degenerated into divorce and eventually to homosexual unions. The modern family is now formless. In the Church, it began with the blurring of the lines of doctrine that led to fuzzy theology and degenerated into faithlessness, into chaos on our campuses, into dull worship and dull Catholics.

The skirmish at the Minneapolis Institute of Arts epito-mizes a much larger problem that can only be solved with the restoration of Catholic culture. Art and morality and religion are all connected. Just as theological ideas must be clear and unambiguous, morality must be well-defined, and artistic lines must be clean and crisp. As Chesterton says, "Art, like morality, consists of drawing the line somewhere."

Chapter Twenty-Eight

THE TRUMPET OF IMAGINATION

The purpose of the imagination is to make us more like God. Sounds like something a serpent might say. But it's not. That really is the purpose of the imagination. To make us more like God. After all, our imagination is a gift from God. It is perhaps one of the greatest gifts God has given us. It not only separates us from the beasts, it allows us to create new worlds of our own. Our imagination gives us a kind of omnipotence. There is almost nothing that we cannot do within the infinity of our minds. The Creator has made us in His own image. That is, he has made us creators. Our creativity is re-creation. And yes, it is recreation as well. It is restorative and rejuvenating. It is a pleasure. It is peace. It is a gift that we have abused, but perhaps even worse, it is a gift we have left unused.

G.K. Chesterton says that imagination is perhaps the mightiest of the pleasures of man. But what is the use of these images that we make inside our heads?

Our first use of imagination, chronologically, that is, comes in the nursery. The four walls, within which we find ourselves as children, seem to be filled with endless worlds of adventure. Fairy tales serve an important role in our imagination. Left to ourselves, our imagination can go astray, even very early on. The fairy tales are the first way we are put on the right track. As Chesterton says:

Fairy tales do not give the child the idea of the evil or the ugly; that is in the child already, because it is in the world already. Fairy tales do not give a child his first idea of bogey. What fairy tales give the child is his first clear idea of the possible defeat of bogey. The baby has known the dragon intimately ever since he had an imagination. What the fairy tale provides for him is a St. George to kill the dragon.

According to Chesterton, imagination is the most essential element in education, and it is the most important product of education. If we learn to use our imaginations, it gives us a certain freedom and self-sufficiency and contentment. "The man who can make up stories about the next-door neighbour will be less-dependent on the next day's newspaper." People who neglect their powers of imagination become both passive and restless. They rely on something else to entertain them, something else to occupy their minds. They are unable to do it themselves. Chesterton says that a society that pays others to dance for them is in a state of decadence. Soon we are paying others to think for us.

Perhaps the most important use of imagination is that it keeps us from going insane. Chesterton says the madman is not the man who has lost his reason. The madman is the man who has lost everything *except* his reason. What he has lost is that human variable that is the creative imagination. The poet, says Chesterton, simply tries to get his head into the heavens, while the logician tries to get the heavens into his head. It is his head that splits.

Along the same lines, Chesterton claims that logic is not a productive tool. It is merely a weapon of defense. We can argue with our opponents using logic and we can certainly defend the truth with it, but we need more than logic to complete our philosophy. He says that we have to be like Nehemiah, the Old Testament hero who rebuilt the walls of Jerusalem. Each of his workers had a sword in one hand and a trowel in the other. The sword was the weapon of defense. The trowel was the creative tool. "The imagination, the constructive quality, is the trowel, and argument is the sword."

Imagination, then, corresponds to faith, as logic does to reason. And just as we cannot lose our imagination, neither can we lose our reason. Reason and Imagination must go together. Our mental and spiritual health depends on keeping this balance. We must have an imaginative use of reason, and a reasonable use of imagination. Without reason, the imagination merely runs wild and goes to weeds. Without imagination, reason is sterile. Chesterton says, "Imagination is a thing of clear images, and the more a thing becomes vague the less imaginative it is. Similarly, the more a thing becomes wild and lawless the less imaginative it is."

The right use of imagination then, is to be lawful, not lawless; to be obedient, not disobedient, to use our creativity for worshipping the Creator, not for defying him. Worship is an act of awe. Artists who have detached themselves from a religious grounding don't fly, but merely float away. Their creativity has no reference point. They try to be original. They try to be different. They try to shock. But endless shock merely makes us senseless. We have lost our true appreciation of surprise because we have the purpose of creativity precisely backwards. "The function of imagination," says Chesterton, "is not to make strange things settled, so much as to make settled things strange; not so much to make wonders facts as to make facts wonders."

Art, like love, is not for ourselves alone. It is first for God, and then for our neighbor. The greatest art helps lift our neighbors to God, even our neighbors who have not been born yet. It is not a passing thrill, but an inspiration for the ages.

"The trumpet of imagination," says Chesterton, "like the trumpet of the Resurrection, calls the dead out of their graves."

Chapter Twenty-Nine

THE FACE OF GOD

There is one group of people who think about God more than
the rest of us do. I'm referring, of course, to atheists. Their minds
are constantly occupied by the God whose existence they are
trying to disprove. But they are such a small minority that their
obsession does not have a significant impact on the world other
than a few irritations regarding what kind of art can be erected in
public buildings and what songs can be sung at winter concerts
during the school year. More troublesome than atheists are the
legions of people who do not think about God at all. They do
not think about God not because they do not believe in him,
but because they do. They do not want to face that fact. They
certainly do not want to face God's face. Many of the world's
problems are caused by the many people who are running away
from God, much more than the few who are running after God.

There is another group. A significant group. They are the
people who heartily and sincerely believe in God, but do not
believe in Christ. They are aware of the claims of Christianity,
but they have pointedly and deliberately rejected them.

My sister-in-law once told me of a discussion she had with
a Jewish man. She asked him why he did not believe that Jesus
was the Son of God. Why could he not admit that Jesus was
the Christ, the fulfillment of all the prophecies in the Hebrew
scripture? His response was this: the Christian view of Jesus as

God in the Flesh directly contradicts the description of God in the Torah. On Mount Sinai, God said to Moses: "You cannot see My face, for no man can see Me and live!" (Ex. 33:20) Thus, Jesus, who claimed that to see him was to see God, could not be God. Because no man can look at God in the face and live.

This seems to be a strong argument, both scripturally and logically. Seems to be. But as it turns out, both scripture and logic contradict it.

There are accounts in the Bible of men who saw God and lived. There was Jacob, who wrestled all night long with an angel. In the morning the angel gave him a new name: Israel, which means "The One Who Struggles with God." At the conclusion of this divine visitation, Jacob built a monument and named the place Penuel, which means "The Face of God," and he said, "I have seen God face to face, yet my life has been preserved." (Gen. 32:30)

There was also the prophet Isaiah who wrote: "In the year that King Uzziah died I saw the Lord sitting upon a throne, high and lifted up; and his train filled the temple." (Is. 6:1) Isaiah was obviously familiar with what God said to Moses because his reaction was "Woe is me! For I am lost…for my eyes have seen the King, the Lord of hosts!" (Is. 6:5) But he survived.

So why is it that looking God in the face has such lethal qualities? The answer should be pretty obvious.

When Adam was in a sinless state, he enjoyed the presence of God, walking with him in the Garden of Eden. When Adam sinned, he heard God walking in the garden and he hid himself. He could not bear to face God or to have God see him. Sin cannot abide in the presence of God. (That is why we should not take communion in the state of mortal sin. It is the sin that will destroy us.)

The Psalms are filled with longing for God, the deep desire to enjoy the fullness and satisfaction of God's presence. In Psalm

27, David prays: "One thing I ask of the Lord, this is what I seek: that I may dwell in the house of the Lord all the days of my life, to gaze upon the beauty of the Lord and to seek him in his temple… My heart says of you, "Seek his face!" Your face, Lord, I will seek. Do not hide your face from me… (Ps. 27: 4,8)

But when David has sinned, he prays just the opposite: "Hide your face from my sin." (Ps. 51:9)

It is the man free from sin who seeks God's face. "For the Lord is righteous, he loves justice; upright men will see his face." (Ps. 11:7) It is the sinner who hides from God's face.

We see the same reaction in the New Testament. When Simon Peter realizes that Jesus is divine, his reaction is not what we might expect. He falls at Jesus' knees and says, "Go away from me, Lord; I am a sinful man!" (Luke 5:8) Children, however, are naturally attracted to Jesus in the Gospel accounts. That is because, as G.K. Chesterton explains, "Children are innocent and love justice; while most of us are wicked and naturally prefer mercy."

But as the Gospels make clear, Jesus came not to judge the world, but to save the world. His divine claim—"Anyone who has seen me has seen the Father" (John 14:9)—infuriates the religious leaders of his day. He audaciously prefaces his miracles with "Your sins are forgiven," but then demonstrates his authority by performing the miracle. He comes as a healer. He is on a mission of mercy, to forgive sins so that everyone can be reconciled to God, so that everyone can see the face of God. But there are some who have no desire for his mercy. And they find only his wrath. They cannot abide this man's claims to forgive sin, to be the fulfillment of the prophets, to be the Son of God. They cannot abide looking God in the face. But they do not run from him; they kill him.

But Christ's death is precisely the sacrifice that takes away the sin of the world. And thus we can look into the face of Christ and see God's love and forgiveness.

As Chesterton intriguingly points out, there is something that the Gospels never reveal about Jesus. His mirth. Chesterton suggests that it is the joy of God that we are unable to bear even more than the wrath or the tears that he did in fact reveal during his time on earth. There is, Chesterton muses, laughter on the secret face of God. There remains something that is too good to be seen, something that will be finally revealed when, as St. Paul promises, we shall no longer be peering through a glass darkly, but shall see Him face to face.

Chapter Thirty

IN THE PRESENCE OF MY ENEMIES

The 23rd Psalm is certainly the most well-known of all the Psalms, and there is nothing wrong with quoting it in full:

> The Lord is my Shepherd; I shall not want.
> He makes me lie down in green pastures.
> He leads me beside still waters.
> He restores my soul.
> He leads me in paths of righteousness for His Name's sake.
> Even though I walk through the valley of the shadow of death,
> I will fear no evil,
> For You are with me.
> Your rod and Your staff comfort me.
> You prepare a table before me in the presence of my enemies.
> You anoint my head with oil.
> My cup overflows.
> Surely goodness and mercy will follow me all the days of my life.
> And I will dwell in the House of the Lord forever.

If we meditate on this wonderful Psalm, we are edified. Simply reading it aloud is like going on a mini spiritual retreat. It is about peace and comfort and renewal. God provides, He protects, He promises life everlasting.

But there is one verse that is really quite startling. Perhaps we have heard it so many times we don't think about it. But if we *do* think about, it seems out of place in this soothing Psalm:

"You prepare a table before me in the presence of my enemies."

What does *that* mean? With all that peace and comfort and joy and abundance, why would we want to have a table prepared for us in the presence of our enemies? Wouldn't we prefer a table with friends and family?

Certainly. But this Psalm is not about we want. It is about what God wants. Right at the beginning we are reminded: "I shall not want." God knows what we need and will provide so that we have no reason to want. There is nothing more fulfilling than matching our desires with God's desires. God has even greater desires for us than we have for ourselves. And certainly more surprising desires. One of those desires is to send us into the presence of our enemies. But he sends us with the promise of protection. "I will fear no evil." ("Be not afraid," says Jesus.) We can walk into the enemy camp without fear and with utter confidence. Even with comfort.

We live in a society that is often hostile to the Catholic faith. Standing up for it is usually unpopular; sometimes it is even dangerous. But when we make our profession of faith, we had better be serious about it. We had better ask ourselves: Do we really believe the thing we're saying? Are we willing to die for it? Are we willing to do the even more difficult thing: to *live* for it, to present ourselves, as St. Paul says, as a *living* sacrifice, which may mean facing daily ridicule, daily suffering, daily setbacks? And there is a more difficult challenge still: Are we willing to do it *with joy*? Are we willing to face our enemies *with joy*?

It is not our enemies who are putting us to the test. It is God. It is God, as the Psalm points out, who prepares the table for us in the presence of our enemies. If we are obedient and faithful, something amazing happens. We are not only *willing* to face our enemies; we find that is a *pleasure* to face them, a joy.

There was one great Christian warrior who seemed to demonstrate the truth of this mysterious passage. Guess who I'm talking about? That's right! G.K. Chesterton. He certainly knew how to dine in the presence of his enemies. He did it quite literally. Chesterton's ideas were diametrically opposed to those of the leading thinkers of the early 20th century, but he had great affection for his opponents, and he invited them to his table as they invited him to theirs. They ate and drank together, and he argued with them deep into the night. Sometimes he convinced them, sometimes he converted them, but even when they remained unconvinced and unconverted, they remained respectful of Chesterton's faith. The notorious skeptic and philanderer H.G. Wells once said that if he had any hope of getting into heaven it would be because he was a friend of Chesterton.

It is Chesterton, of course, who says the Bible teaches us to love our neighbors and love our enemies because generally they are the same people! But the charge to love our enemies has a simple, practical effect: by loving our enemies we can change them into our friends. Think about it: if we obey the command to love our enemies, then by sitting down at the table with our enemies, we are with those we love!

If we have confidence in the truth, we cannot be threatened. If we appreciate the gift of life God has given us, we cannot be uncomfortable with anything that life offers. And finally, if we are willing to fight for the truth, there is no better way to do it than on the bloodless battlefield of the dinner table, clashing the intellectual swords, conquering new territory while performing works of charity, with goblet full to overflowing.

Chapter Thirty-One

WHAT IS A HERETIC?

Among the many clear and concise words that we can no longer use is the word "heretic." Well, we can use it, but only to refer to how that Big Bad Catholic Church burned all those good, well-meaning folks throughout history after labeling them as heretics. Obviously, to use the word now means that we are planning a public execution of some innocent person.

But G.K. Chesterton had no hesitation in calling people heretics. In fact, he even called some of his best friends heretics. And interestingly enough, at the time he was writing, certain skeptics were actually starting to take pride in being known as heretics. It had for them the refreshing and cavalier sensation of being a rebel.

But that is not what a heretic is. A heretic is simply an incomplete thinker. It is someone who has chosen part of the truth, and taken that partial truth and exalted it above the whole truth, even to the point of using the partial truth against the whole truth. A heretic is someone who is truly narrow-minded, and sometimes dangerously narrow-minded. He is trapped, as Chesterton says, "in the clean, well-lit prison of one idea."

Chesterton is a complete thinker. It is one of the reasons he can write about everything. It is one of the reasons he appeals to such a wide variety of people. Truth is broad; heresy is narrow.

It is also why he is so good at exposing heresy. The complete truth recognizes partial truths, not the other way around.

The modern heresies attempt to interpret all reality through the limited lens of a particular theory or discipline. The Darwinists try to explain everything in terms of biology. The Marxists try to explain everything in terms of economics. The Freudians try to explain everything in terms of sex. They are almost laughably narrow, but we cannot laugh because too many people have suffered both in mind and body from these bad ideas.

The ancient heresies, which are old, but still around, usually involve an incomplete understanding of Christ. The Incarnation is the central truth of our faith: the doctrine that Christ is fully God and fully man. The typical heretic of the ancient variety chooses one aspect of Christ over the other, making Jesus either too human or too divine, losing the paradoxical balance of The Word Made Flesh.

In between the ancient heresies and the modern secular heresies are the Protestant heresies. Each Protestant "sect" is called a sect because it is indeed a "section" of something larger. That larger thing is the Catholic Church. Shortly after I became a Catholic, I was talking with a Catholic woman who said she had always wanted to find out more about the different Protestant churches. I told her that all she had to do was take the Catholic Church and start cutting parts of it away. That is basically what each Protestant sect is. Each has kept something, but has left out something greater. Some have, for instance, kept the Bible, but have left out the authority of the Church, which gave us the Canon of Scripture. In some cases, they have kept the sovereignty of God, but left out free will. They have kept heaven, but left out hell. They have kept the Virgin Birth, but left out the Mother of God. And they have kept the homily, but left out the priest. What most Protestant converts finally realize is that their church has something it still calls an altar, but nothing called a sacrifice, which is the only thing an altar is used for.

Chesterton marvelously illustrates this idea in—where else?—one of his *Illustrated London News* essays. He says that a man who builds a pile of stones and burns a sacrifice to his god is obviously doing a religious act. It makes sense that over time, others would come and participate in such a sacred ceremony, and that he might give them benches to sit on and build a roof for them to keep them out of the rain, and he might turn some of his prayers into ordered chants that can be repeated, and he might take the opportunity to address the other people and explain what he is doing, and write down the prayers and the chants in a book and place the book on a lectern from which to read it to the others. But in any case, no matter what is added to the religious act, it is clear what the religious act is.

So what do the reformers do? They don't take away all the additions. They leave the hard benches and the lectern. They take away the real religious thing. They take away the altar. They take away the sacrifice. They take away the God.

In most cases, it is not what heretics add that gets them into trouble; it is what they take away. It is not so much that they believe a lie, but that they settle for something less than the whole truth. They prefer the tiny bit of truth they have kept to the gigantic truth they have left behind.

Chapter Thirty-Two

WHAT IS THE IMPORTANCE OF RITUAL?

How many times have you heard the criticism that there are too many rituals in the Catholic Church? Or that the Catholic Church is nothing but rituals? Or that the Catholic Church would be a lot better if it got rid of all the rituals?

Whatever the objection about rituals, they have one thing in common: the people making the objection have not really thought about what they are saying. Though they have taken the trouble to complain about the Catholic rituals, they have not taken the further trouble to consider the purpose of rituals in general, in the Church or anywhere else. They claim they want to do away with the rituals in the Catholic Church, but they certainly are not willing to do away with the rituals in their daily lives. They still shake hands when they meet people, they still sign their names on documents, and they still applaud at concerts. They still have birthday parties with cake and candles and confetti. They still put the word "welcome" on doormats and still put doorknockers on doors. Men still wear neckties when they are told to, and even bow ties when they are told to. Women still put on elaborate wedding dresses and march slowly down the aisle accompanied by carefully selected music and stand before a figure in whom some authority has been invested by some other authority through some sort of ritual. Some men even still open doors for some women. We are all ritualists, says Chesterton, but we are either conscious or unconscious ritualists.

A ritual is something simple used to represent something more complex. We shake hands to indicate that we are friendly rather than trying to explain this generous state of mind. We present a birthday cake to explain our appreciation that a certain person was born and is in fact still alive. We scribble our names on a document to demonstrate that what is written there is something that we agree to. Every symbol means something. Every symbol is a form of shorthand to convey a more elaborate meaning as quickly and succinctly as possible.

As Chesterton explains: "Symbolism and ritual keep things much simpler than they would otherwise be. The natural tendency of all things in a civilized state is to grow more and more complicated. The only way to keep them at all simple is to fix them forever in one form; that is, to make them a ceremony."

If we abolish ritual, we end up replacing it with an inferior ritual. "Destroy your impressive ceremony, and all you get in return is an unimpressive ceremony."

But the object of a ceremony, he says, is not to be beautiful, though that is a valuable element. "The object of a ceremony is to be ceremonious. Ritual is a need of the human soul—nay, it is rather a need of the human body, like exercise."

The ceremonies in the Catholic Church address this very basic human need for the ceremonial. In meeting this need, Chesterton says that the Church decided that the ceremonies should be gorgeous rather than threadbare or third-rate. "Rome had to decide whether it would express the simplicity of Christ in simplicity or the glory of God in glory." Those who objected to the ritual and who abolished the ritual have merely replaced it with inferior ritual. The beautiful art and architecture, the statuary, the music and chants and prayers and vestments and postures have all been replaced with inferior versions, in some cases vastly inferior.

For those who claim that there is too much theatre in Catholic ritual, they should be advised that theatre itself began as a religious ritual. Greek worshippers wanted to "act out" their devotion to their gods. The acting became a form of story-telling, and the stories became more varied, but at the heart of it was a group of people performing, that is, taking the form of something other than themselves, something beyond themselves. The ancient Greek actors performed with great excitement. There was a word to describe their intensity and zeal and passion. The word is enthusiasm. It meant literally that God was inside of them.

It is true that most people don't understand the meaning of all the rituals in the Catholic Church, including many Catholics themselves. If they did understand them, they would have a deeper appreciation and a more profound experience of worship every time a vested priest entered the church, every time a book was held high, was kissed, was opened, every time a knee was bent, a head was bowed, every time bread and wine was carried forward to the front of the sanctuary. Every color, every gesture, every item used is "significant," that is, it means something and it is important. To learn what it all means is fascinating and exciting, and it makes the rituals themselves fascinating and exciting.

At the high point of our ritual, we eat God's body and drink his blood. But where is our excitement over this astonishing act? Perhaps this is what leads the casual critics to conclude that our rituals are meaningless and worthless and empty. We claim to believe that when we take the Eucharist, God is literally inside of us. And yet, where is our enthusiasm?

Chapter Thirty-Three

BAD PREACHING

The homily is the least important part of the Mass. But that does not mean it has to be bad. Yet so many of them *are* bad. Why is that?

One reason is that the priest is perhaps under the mistaken impression that the homily is the *most* important part of the Mass. If that's the case, he may as well go over to the Protestant church across the street, where the service consists almost entirely of a sermon garnished with a few songs and prayers and announcements.

But there is another reason why homilies are bad, and we can see the reason if we take a look at the Protestant churches, where the sermons are often quite good.

The sermons in a conservative Protestant church, such as an evangelical Baptist congregation, are usually going to be interesting and inspiring and even entertaining because there is a clearly defined theology that is being preached. There is a definite theoretical form to follow and an endless wealth of material to draw from. The theoretical form is Christian. The source material is the Bible. There is a strong doctrine and a strong morality that flows from it. There are truths to be proclaimed and sins to be condemned. And the preaching that goes along with it will be strong.

These preachers look at St. Peter and St. Paul primarily as fellow preachers. They also emphasize Christ's preaching, sometimes even more than the Incarnation and the Crucifixion. But because they believe something, they can articulate it very well and they can talk about how it relates to everything else. And they will never run out of something to preach about. Chesterton muses that watching these preachers is sometimes like watching an acrobat, but there is real fun because there is real thinking. There is real thinking because there is real theology.

But there is no sacrament. There is only a sermon. It is often a very good sermon. It had better be. It is basically the only reason to attend that church.

On the other hand, in a liberal Protestant church, that is, a washed-out, so-called mainstream congregation, where textual criticism has emptied the Bible of its meaning, where "progressive" is the keyword and "traditional" is anathema, where there is no clear doctrine and an even less clear morality, the sermon is going to be boring. Chesterton says, "The parson is not dull because he is always expounding theology, but because he has no theology to expound." There may be some passionate pleas about social justice, but there is no theoretical basis to justify the justice. These are Christian churches that seem to be embarrassed by Christianity. The pastors will announce that they cannot know the truth, and then will complain if anyone else claims to know the truth. They have nothing to say, and complain if someone else says something.

They rely only on sentimentality. They avoid definitions because definitions have boundaries and might leave someone out. They have no creed. They have no theology. Theology, even bad theology, has some logic to it, and logic is a tool that always stands ready to use. But emotion is fugitive. Feelings are fleeting and formless, and it takes a great effort to whip them up. All this appealing only to the heart, and never to the head, just creates a lot of froth.

Chesterton says that this broad-minded, doctrine-avoiding kind of preacher really has nothing to preach about: "He is to give us every Sunday his own hazy feelings about humanity, because he has no moral system to apply to particular human problems. These sentimentalists ... have themselves created the very ineptitude of which they complain..." He says they merely want to prove their large-mindedness by talking at large. But they do not know what they want. "They do not even know that in some feeble fashion they want Protestantism to drift into Pantheism." A Chestertonian prophecy of the modern Cult of Inclusiveness.

Now, what we see across the Protestant spectrum is unfortunately true within the Catholic Church. The priest who takes the Catholic creed seriously, who understands Catholic theology, who closely adheres to the Church's teachings on faith and morals, will have no trouble giving a good homily at every single Mass. The readings provide rich material of which we need constantly to be reminded. They are old truths that always sound new because they always matter in our daily lives. And even if the homily is not exciting or emotional, it simply has to be true; its main function is to support the rest of the liturgy. And the main purpose of the liturgy is the celebration of the Eucharist. We do not go to Church to hear a sermon. We go to receive the Body of Christ. Everything else is there to support that central truth. If the structure holding it up is strong that truth will not collapse.

In Catholic parishes where the doctrine is openly doubted, where traditional morals are questioned or even sneered at, where the faith is not a foundation but an inconvenience and even an embarrassment, the homilies will be dreadful. They might be passionate, they might be emotional, but unless they are merely angry, they will probably be neither. In any case, they will be a distraction from the Eucharist. The whole structure is weakened. The whole liturgy will take second place to the sermon. And in all likelihood the liturgy will be tinkered with and toyed with, and soon made as formless as the theology it reflects.

The sad thing is that it is so easy to do things right. The Church has given us a clear form to follow. It has given us a theoretical system that explains everything. There are still mysteries, and it is always a rich and profound experience to meditate on these mysteries, but only because the truth is a deep well that is always satisfying and never runs dry, not because it is simply an impenetrable fog in which we are merely lost.

Chapter Thirty-Four

THE DEVIL KNOWS SCRIPTURE

One of the greatest arguments against the doctrine of *Sola Scriptura* comes from Scripture. In Matthew 4 we learn that the earliest proponent of the idea of using the Bible as the sole authority is … Satan. When Christ faces Satan in the desert, the devil tries to tempt Jesus by quoting Scripture. Let's see you jump off the temple. The angels will protect you, won't they? Says so right in the Psalms.

A person with merely the Bible as his guide might be tempted to try it. But a wiser believer knows there is more to revealed truth than what is written in the sacred texts. This takes nothing away from Scripture; on the contrary, it strengthens it. It nourishes it. But it is more important to be grounded in the Truth than to be grounded in the Bible. As in the Parable of the Sower, unless the seed (which is the Word of God) falls on good soil, it will be not take proper root and it will not be fruitful. It will either whither in the rocks or be choked by the thorns or be snatched away by the birds.

Quoting Scripture to tempt the faithful is a technique that the devil has made great use of throughout history. Not only did it give rise to Martin Luther's complete break with the Roman Catholic Church, it continued to weaken all of Christendom, as each new Protestant sect broke away from the sect set up by its rebellious forefathers. The issue was always over different interpretations of different verses. The endless splintering led to over 20,000 Christian denominations, some of which are barely recognizable as Christian, though they still cling to one or two Biblical passages when it suits them.

Satan still uses this technique to lead the faithful astray. "The devil can quote Scripture for his purpose," says Chesterton, "and the text of Scripture which he now most commonly quotes is, 'The kingdom of heaven is within you.'" This provocative and suggestive Bible verse points to our responsibility and freedom to obey and to fulfill our various callings. Why does the devil quote this passage? Because, taken out of context, it is a verse that can do more harm than good, more destruction to the kingdom of heaven than any building up of it.

By itself, it implies that we are by ourselves, that we do not need any outside help, that the truth is merely internal and subjective, that we make our own truth, and that it is not important what our parents tell us, what the prophets tell us, what the saints tell us, what the Church tells us. And it leads to the dangerous and destructive conclusion that whatever is within us is the truth.

We see this in everything from New Age religions to Secular Self-Help Seminars, with the mantra of "looking within yourself" and drawing on "the inner power" rather than seeking the higher power which is God. But as Chesterton says, "I do not in my private capacity believe that a baby gets his best physical food by sucking his thumb; nor that a man gets his best moral food by sucking his soul, and denying its dependence on God or other good things."

Truth comes from outside of us. That is why it is called "good news" It is something we hear told to us. Jesus says, "He who has ears to hear, let him hear."

But the devil cleverly uses part of the good news as a means of deception: we can suddenly get stuck on the idea that the

Kingdom of Heaven is merely within us. As Chesterton points out, this is the weak spot in the soul of our age that the devil seizes upon. We are drawn to the idea that we do not need the external truths as long as our heart is right, that as long as we get the "spirit" of a thing, we don't need the letter of it. How often have we seen changes to the teachings and practices of the Church, in the liturgy and so on that have been invoked or inflicted "in the spirit of Vatican II"? Whenever you hear someone use this phrase to justify something, you can be sure of one thing: that person has never read a single document from the Second Vatican Council.

When St. Paul warned that the letter of the law kills, while the spirit gives life, he did not mean that the letter of the law must be tossed out and only the spirit retained. He was warning against legalism, which is a spiritless understanding of the Law of God. He was insisting on the *sacramental* nature of truth: that it is both spiritual and physical, both internal and external. It is not merely one or the other it is both.

If the Kingdom is merely inside us, if we neglect the external, we neglect putting our faith into practice. There is no evidence of our faith. We are invisible.

The devil is devious. He uses this text to attack the distinct element of the Catholic faith: the Sacraments.

When we neglect the external practice of our faith, the forms, the structure, the tangible, we will neglect the internal truth right along with it. When we neglect baptism and confirmation, we neglect the faith that follows them. When we neglect the marriage vows, we neglect purity and chastity. When we neglect the priestly vows, we neglect the souls that depend on them. When we neglect penance, we neglect confession, we neglect contrition. Ironically, the most obvious evidence of truth inside of us is when we confess our sins.

And then there is the neglecting of the Eucharist. If we do not attend Mass, the rest of our lives suffer. If we neglect the proper form of the liturgy, error rushes in. If we neglect to take the Sacrament seriously, we trivialize Christ on the Cross and the Supreme Sacrifice of God Himself.

The word "Eucharist" literally means thanksgiving. Thankfulness is not possible if truth is merely within us. We must have something to be thankful *to*. It is a logical impossibility to be thankful without being able to give thanks to something outside of ourselves. The Kingdom of Heaven is within us because it is thankfulness that comes out of us; it is our love for God, which opens our hearts to his blessings. Chesterton says, "Everything is blessed from beyond, by something which has in its turn been blessed from beyond again: only the blessed bless."

※

Chapter Thirty Five

A LESSON FROM ESTHER

Here is a trivia question: What is the only book in the Bible that does not mention God?

If you are a Protestant, you will answer: "Esther." If you are a Catholic, you will answer: "All of the books in the Bible mention God."

Okay, what's going on? How can we have two different answers?

This is how it happened. When the Protestant reformers developed their *Sola Scriptura* theology—the idea that the Bible, not the Church, was the ultimate authority in matters of doctrine and faith—before they ceded all that power over to the Scriptures, they first made an adjustment to the Scriptures, based on their own authority. They threw out certain books of the Bible. Although Martin Luther wanted to jettison James and Revelation, the New Testament managed to stay intact, but in the Old Testament several books—Tobit, Judith, Wisdom, Sirach, Baruch, I and II Maccabees—lost their status as Scripture. Part of the argument was that these books had no identifiable versions in the original Hebrew, but only existed in the Greek version known as the Septuagint (which is the version of the Old Testament that is quoted in the New Testament). Most Jewish scripture scholars from the Second Century and following did not consider these books to be part of the Hebrew Bible. But it is quite possible that part of their reason for rejecting these books had nothing to do with the lack of original Hebrew manuscripts, but was instead a reaction to the Christians who had not only accepted these books as Scripture, but were using them to demonstrate that Jesus was the Messiah. It is interesting that these Jewish scholars and rabbis decided to clean up the canon a hundred years after Christ had come.

Then, over a thousand years later, along came the reformers, and oddly enough, they sided with the Jews rather than with the Church on which books should be included in the Old Testament. It might also be pointed out that the books they rejected contained a great deal of the Scriptural basis for certain Catholic doctrines such as Purgatory and the honored tradition of praying for the dead. If your Biblical Theology does not include Purgatory, it is helpful to eliminate Biblical references that support the doctrine of Purgatory. And so on.

What does this have to do with Esther? Because the Deutero-Canonicals (those parts of the Bible that the Catholic Church believes to be inspired but the Protestants do not) include portions of Old Testament books that were kept by the Catholic Church but not by the reformers. These include parts of Esther and Daniel. The portions from Esther contain several beautiful prayers imploring God's help in a time of great testing and trial. These prayers do not appear in the Protestant Bibles, and so, yes, they have a book in their Bibles that does not mention God. Their loss. The irony, I suppose, is that the *Sola Scriptura* people actually removed God from one of the books of the Bible!

But the reason I bring up Esther has nothing to do with that long-winded introduction. It has to do with the much more profound subject of doing God's Will.

When we are called to do God's Will, what happens if we disobey? What happens, that is, (a.) to us, and (b.) to God's will? Do we thwart his plan? Do we prevent God's Will from being carried out? It is an interesting question, and the answer, I think, is revealed in the Book of Esther.

The story concerns the Jews in exile in Persia who are threatened to be annihilated because of the treachery of a royal official named Haman. But the King, Ahasuerus, has married a beautiful young Jewish woman named Esther, and her cousin Mordecai appeals to her to go before the King and save the Jews from destruction. She is afraid because no one, not even the Queen, may appear before the King unsummoned. The penalty is death. But Mordecai, a godly man, tells Esther: "If you keep silence at such a time as this, relief and deliverance will rise for the Jews from another quarter, but you and your father's house will perish. And who knows whether you have not come to the kingdom for such a time as this?" (4:14)

In other words, God gives us great opportunities to carry out his will, and if we disobey, God's Will shall be accomplished by another means, probably through another person's obedience. If we disobey, we will not only be deprived of blessings meant for us, but suffer the horrible consequences of disobedience: possibly losing everything, including life itself. The wages of sin is death.

This Biblical lesson is reinforced by the saints. We see it in a prayer by St. John Chrysostom: "Lord, Thou knowest that Thou dost as Thou Willest, let then Thy will be done in me, sinner, for blessed art Thou unto the Ages, Amen."

I remember Mother Teresa of Calcutta saying that she was not the best person suited to do the work she was doing as a Missionary of Charity, that she was just filling in until God would bring along someone more obedient, more humble. Though this is not imaginable to us, we see that this saint answered a call that perhaps was made to someone else before her but would certainly be made to someone else after her. She knew that God's Will did not depend on her, but she knew that she had the privilege of helping carry out God's Will, even if she felt unworthy of that role.

We could all do with a little more of such humility and faith and obedience.

Chapter Thirty-Six

A LESSON FROM ST. JAMES

It can't be a comfortable feeling when you base your theology only on the Bible, and then find that the Bible contradicts your theology. That was the ticklish position in which Martin Luther found himself. His surprising solution was to keep the theology and toss out the Bible, or at least the parts of the Bible that did not jive with his theology. Out went the books of Maccabees and all that nonsense about praying for the dead (because there can't be a purgatory—either you are saved or you are not). Out went Sirach and all that mumbo jumbo about priests and garments and silver chalices (because we don't need all those rituals in our worship). Out went Tobit with that made-up stuff about the angel Raphael (because, well, that's what Catholics believe), and all that unnecessary emphasis on behaving yourself (because we are saved by faith alone). These books of the Bible became known as the Apocrypha, which means the authenticity of their authorship was "doubtful." But when you begin to doubt scripture, where do you stop? When the Protestants consigned part of the Bible to the dustbin of the Apocrypha, something happened that they did not anticipate. Other doubters stepped forward and began doubting the rest of the Bible as well. This skepticism grew like a cancer, and in its advanced stages it took on the form of "textual criticism" and "deconstruction" from scholars who eventually determined that basically nothing in the Bible is reliable. It is either borrowed or stolen or invented or interpolated. As Chesterton observes of this amazing academic vandalism, the critics determined that the books of Moses were not written by Moses but by someone else of the same name.

There was another book that Martin Luther also wanted to excise from the Bible: the Epistle of St. James. The sum of Luther's theology is that a man is justified by faith alone. But the only place in the Bible where the words "faith" and "alone" appear together is in the second chapter of St. James: "So you see, a man is justified by works, and not by faith alone." There could not possibly be a clearer, cleaner contradiction of Martin Luther than in that one verse. Which is why Luther wanted to jettison James. But getting rid of New Testament books was not as simple as getting rid of Old Testament books, especially one written by an Apostle. James had to stay. But Luther grumbled nonetheless, calling it "that epistle of straw." Interestingly enough, the Epistle of St. James also warns against grumbling.

Now, as tempting as it is to use St. James simply for the purpose of picking on poor Martin Luther and dismantling the primary parts of Protestant theology, I think the importance of this book is even more for Catholics than for Protestants. There is hardly a more Catholic book in the Bible than St. James. It would be a good exercise to sit and read these five chapters once a week and make them part of our daily meditation. The lessons therein are, to put it mildly, eternally valuable.

James tells us to be joyful in suffering, to avoid doubt and double-mindedness, to take responsibility for our own sins, to be "quick to hear, slow to speak, and slow to anger." He reminds us that every gift comes from God, that mercy triumphs over judgment, that God opposes the proud but gives grace to the humble. He exhorts us to be doers of the word and not hearers only, which means visiting orphans and widows in their affliction and showing no partiality, and paying the worker a just wage. All edifying.

But there is one passage that very pointedly addresses some of the main problems we are facing in the Church today:

> Who is wise and understanding among you? By his good life let him show his works in the meekness of wisdom. But if you have bitter jealousy and selfish ambition in your hearts, do not boast and be false to the truth. This wisdom is not such as comes down from above, but is earthly, unspiritual and devilish. For where jealousy and selfish ambition exist there will be disorder and every vile practice. But the wisdom from above is first pure, then peaceable, gentle, open to reason, full of mercy and good fruits, without uncertainty or insincerity. And the harvest of righteousness is sown in peace by those who make peace.[1]

All of the dissent and dissatisfaction within the Church— whether it be from feminists who do not understand the priest- hood or homosexuals who do not understand marriage or theology professors who do not understand authority—all of it boils down to the problem explained in these verses: it is the result of bitter jealousy and selfish ambition. They are all proud, and they are false to the truth. Theirs is not the wisdom that comes from above, and, worst of all, their attitudes and actions lead to disorder and every vile practice. But the proper way to deal with them is not to attack them viciously, but first of all to live the right kind of life ourselves, to show our good works in the *meekness* of wisdom, and then demonstrate a wisdom that is pure, peaceable, gentle, open to reason, full of mercy and

---

[1] The Epistle of Saint James 3:12-18. Holy Bible Revised Standard Version Catholic Edition (Ignatius Press: San Francisco, 1994).

good fruits, without uncertainty or insincerity. That is how we make peace.

And it is important that we make peace with those who want to disrupt the Church. It is important for the obvious reason that those who have strayed from the truth are in great peril. The Epistle of St. James ends by urging us to bring back those people from the error of their ways. Because by doing so, we will "save their souls from death and cover a multitude of sins."

Chapter Thirty-Seven

A COMMENTARY ON BIBLE COMMENTARIES

When I was a Baptist who believed that the Bible was the only authority, I was always very keen on reading and studying scripture. I knew my Bible very well—and still do, thankfully. But at that time I also had to read a lot of commentaries on the Bible, since, contrary to what Evangelicals may say, the Bible does not always speak for itself. Believers speak for it. It requires a little elucidation here and there. Even Jesus' disciples asked him to explain what His parables meant. Even St. Peter, while exhorting others to read the epistles of St. Paul, cautioned, "there are some things in them hard to understand." (II Peter 3:16) We use the Psalms in our regular worship, but some of them don't always look so edifying at first glance. What, for instance, do you make of the verse from Psalm 137, where it says, "Happy shall he be who takes your little ones and dashes them against the rock!" Doesn't exactly sound like Christian charity, does it? Doesn't sound too Pro-Life, either. How do you make sense of things like that? Where do you get help?

From the Church. That is where I finally had to go to understand the Bible. I will tell you how I got there.

There are a few people who perhaps suspect that reading G.K. Chesterton might have had something to do with my conversion to the Catholic faith. Well, I confess, it's true. He is a dangerous writer, the way he gets people to think about things that they were sure they were never going to think about. And while my debt to Chesterton is eternal, I must point out that there were several other writers who helped me along on my path to Rome. Interestingly enough, almost all of these other writers belonged to one group. Discovering this group was like discovering buried treasure. Among their many gifts, I found that their particular strength was Bible commentary. They opened up the scriptures to me in ways that I had never imagined. They deepened the love that I already had for the Word of God, but they added an enormously profound understanding to go with it.

Who were these guys? The Early Church Fathers.

Most of the Bible commentaries that I had read previously had been written in the 20th century. Maybe a few of them went as far back as the 19th century. The Early Church Fathers offered a fresh perspective from the vantage point of many centuries before that, a perspective somewhat closer to the time that the Bible itself was written and less clouded by the reactions to it since.

One of those fathers was St. Jerome, whose intimacy with Scripture was perhaps unmatched, whose knowledge and understanding was no doubt nourished during his astounding translation of both the Old and New Testaments into Latin. What does he have to say, for instance, about that troubling passage from Psalm 137?

> By the waters of Babylon, there we sat down and wept,
> When we remembered Zion.
> On the willows there we hung up our lyres.
> For there our captors required of us songs, and our tormentors,
>   mirth, saying,
> "Sing us one of the songs of Zion!"

How shall we sign the Lord's song in a foreign land?
…O daughter of Babylon, you devastator!
Happy shall he be who requites you with what you done to us!
Happy shall he be who takes your little ones and dashes them
    against the rock!

Jerome points out that the word Babylon means confusion. Hence, he says, "Babylon is a figure of this world. It is the sinner…" The sinner is one who has lost his way. We weep by the waters of Babylon, because we remember our former happiness, before we sinned. We cannot sing the Lord's song in a strange land, that is, we cannot praise God when we are in a sinful state. Sin separates us from God.

Jerome explains that the infants in this Psalm, the "little ones," are sinful thoughts, evil desires that have not yet matured into full-grown sin. "If I do not at once cut off that sinful desire and take hold of it, as it were, by the foot and dash it against a rock until sensual passion abates, it will be too late afterwards when the smoldering fire has burst into flame. Blessed is the man who puts the knife instantly to sinful passion and smashes it against a rock!" The rock, he explains, is Christ. That's where we take our sins to have them destroyed.

So, this famous lament of the Jews in captivity works on many higher (and deeper) levels. As usual, Christ turns up in the Old Testament. As usual, sin prevents us from experiencing full communion with Christ. As usual, Christ helps us overcome sin. But what astonishing insight into this Psalm! What an unforgettable image to inspire us to smash sinful desires before they capture us. The resulting sensation, as the Psalm says, is one of happiness. We are truly happy when we have defeated sin.

St. Jerome was one of many from this group of writers who helped me better understand and appreciate the Bible. As I said, these writers belonged to a group: the Early Church Fathers. But the Early Church Fathers all belonged to the Church. As I read them, it made me long for the Ancient Church. The startling revelation was that the Ancient Church is still here, and still welcoming new members. Also smashed in all this was my old Protestant prejudice that the Catholic Church was somehow against Scripture. The Church that gave us the Bible is still protecting the Bible, and explaining what it means. None of the old truths have died; they have only proven themselves to be eternal.

Chapter Thirty-Eight

AMONG THE EVANGELICALS

I once had the privilege of attending an academic conference on G.K. Chesterton at what would seem to be an unlikely place: a Methodist Theological Seminary in Kentucky. Almost all of the participants in the conference were Evangelical Protestants. One of the questions that came up was, "Why are Evangelicals so drawn towards a writer like G.K. Chesterton?" It is indeed a fascinating question, and even more fascinating to hear it asked in a positive way, in a Southern accent, and in the intonations of a Bible-believing, devil-defying, pulpit-pounding preacher.

It is not strange, of course, that anyone is drawn toward Chesterton. He is a charming, witty, and delightful writer who tells the truth in a compelling way. He is a complete thinker with a complete philosophy that really does have an answer for everything. But he also speaks the truth with a combination of confidence and humility, of joy and satisfaction and wonder, not found in any other modern writer. What really perplexed the participants at this conference was the word they were leaving out of the question they were asking. The complete question was: "Why are Evangelicals so drawn towards a *Catholic* writer like G.K. Chesterton?"

It was one of those rare moments when I kept my mouth shut even though I knew the answer. They may not have been ready to accept the answer from a Catholic, but they were making themselves ready for the answer even by groping for it, even by dancing around the real question. And in the scholarly papers that were presented as well as in the discussion that followed, I heard things that I never would have imagined coming from Evangelicals.

For instance, one professor explained that a century ago, Evangelicals focused on "personalism," the idea that God was a "personal" God and one must have a "personal" relationship with Him. However, thanks to Chesterton (and the Inklings who came after him: C.S. Lewis, J.R.R. Tolkien, Charles Williams, Dorothy L. Sayers), the Evangelicals discovered a deeper and wider understanding of God based on the Trinity. Yes, they were talking about the Trinity as if it were a new theological discovery of the 20th century. The only thing that amazed them was that Chesterton talked about the Trinity before Karl Barth did.

Another professor talked about how the Bible has been under attack by textual critics and by strange scholarly and theological interpretations for a long time. Protestants have been so busy trying to understand the Old Testament as a Hebrew document that they have forgotten to see it as a Christian document. "Have we forgotten our own story?" she asked. She talked about the need to recognize "a Christian Canon." But at the same time, she recognized that such a declaration can only be made by some authority. Yes, they *have* forgotten their own story. They have forgotten that the Canon of Scripture was declared by the Catholic Church, and that the Authority of the Catholic Church was in place before the Canon of Scripture was in place, and that the Catholic Church has always offered the Christian interpretation of the Old Testament. They have forgotten their own story, but by asking the right questions, they were starting to remember.

And in one discussion, someone pointed out that there is a physical, material aspect to the Christian faith, because God came in the flesh. In II Corinthians 4:6 it says that we come to "the Glory of God in the Face of Christ." This is not just a symbol but a reality. So, too, the cross is a symbol but it is also a reality. There was a real cross of real wood that soaked up the real blood of Christ. Yes, without knowing it, they were talking about sacramentals, about the logic of devotions to the Holy Face and to the True Cross.

Another presenter mentioned that the term "orthodoxy" means literally "straight doctrine" but the Greek word, *dox*, which means "doctrine," originally meant "glory" (as in "doxology"). It meant giving thanks and praise to God, which, of course, is the right thing to do, the "orthodox" thing to do. There is a connection between glory and doctrine. Interestingly enough, G.K. Chesterton, the defender of orthodoxy, said, "Thanks is the highest form of thought." And of course, "Eucharist" means "thanksgiving." Yes, without knowing it, they were talking about the importance of "Eucharist."

The word "Catholic" came up a couple times during this conference. It was even mentioned once that the word literally means "according to the whole." The truths that they were trying so hard to articulate were indeed truths "according to the whole" truth. I have no doubt when they left that place they were thinking about the wholeness of the faith that was embraced by G.K. Chesterton, which they, too, wanted to embrace. And they all took a step closer that weekend. My role was only to meekly answer technical questions about Chesterton's writings and to make them all wonder why I seemed so happy.

Protestant sects can only do one of two things. They can begin to recover what they have lost and become more Catholic, or else they can fade away and disappear. They cannot simply remain the same.

This point was illustrated perfectly in another experience I had in Kentucky that same weekend. When I drove across the state, I stopped and visited two very interesting places. One was a historic Shaker Village. The other was a Trappist Monastery. The Shakers were a religious community known for living a simple life. The Trappists are also a religious community who live a simple life. These two places were built about the same time in the middle of the 19th century. But the Shaker Village is a museum. There are no Shakers there anymore. The monastery, however, is still filled with monks, and is doing the exact thing it was doing not only when it was built 150 years ago, but the same thing Trappists have been doing for over 800 years. There was a vivid difference between the two places. The difference between an absence and a presence.

ã

Chapter Thirty-Nine

THE ECUMENICAL MARY

One of the hardest things for Protestant Evangelicals and Fundamentalists to understand is the Catholic devotion to Mary. Believe me. I've been there. For me it was the first and the last hurdle to becoming a Catholic. On the other hand, one of the hardest things for lifelong Catholics to understand is the reluctance, even the sense of repulsion that Protestants have toward this devotion. And so, if Catholics are going to defend their faith and speak the truth in love, they will do well to try to understand the difficulty that their separated brethren have on this important subject.

I believe in true Ecumenism, that is, in emphasizing the things we have in common with other Christians. There is no question that among our most important allies in the culture wars are the Evangelicals, who are as serious as we are about protecting religious freedom, the traditional family, and simple moral decency. They stand with us in the battle we are fighting against obvious evils such as abortion, homosexuality, and pornography, and subtle evils such as relativism, materialism and agnosticism. And I can tell you that they worship God sincerely, they love Christ deeply, and they seek the presence of the Holy Spirit in their lives.

We must not purposely alienate them by emphasizing our differences rather than our shared beliefs. And yet, I truly believe that as Catholics in the New Dark Ages in which we live, the most important thing we can do to strengthen our own faith, to protect our families, and to bring light to the darkness that surrounds us is to increase our devotion to the Mother of God.

Our Protestant friends think that we are seriously off-kilter because we pray to Mary. They think our devotion to her arises out of superstition, goddess worship, or worse. They think our veneration of the Virgin diminishes the role of Christ.

So what do we do?

We need to explain that the Church has had a high view of Mary throughout history, and the Protestant rejection of the role of the Blessed Mother comes late in the history of Christianity, even late in the history of Protestantism. Luther, for instance, believed in the perpetual virginity of Mary, a doctrine later rejected by Lutherans.

In fact, the historical argument, as it usually does, strengthens the defense of any Catholic belief, but especially concerning the reasons for the devotion to Mary. History shows, quite simply, that it is the right thing to do.

In the Dark Ages, there was barely any civilization at all. The only light in the Dark Ages was the Church. And interestingly enough, this was when the devotion to Mary began to grow, and with it, so did the Church grow. That growth carried Christendom into the glorious light of the High Middle Ages. When Christendom found itself under attack by a strangely singular thing called Islam during the Crusades, it was devotion to Mary that built the great Gothic Cathedrals, which still stand as living monuments to the faith. When Christendom was suddenly split apart from within by the Protestant rebellion, it was Catholic soldiers and citizens praying the Rosary that won the Battle of Lepanto and not only saved western civilization but strengthened the decimated Church. When both the Eastern and Protestant iconoclasts began to smash Catholic art, it was devotion to Mary that produced some of the most beautiful images the world has ever known, as Madonnas were painted and sculpted and lit up in stained glass and glorified in song. When anti-clericalism was at its height in the 19th century, Bl. Pope Pius IX declared the Doctrine of the Immaculate Conception, which led to enormous growth in the Catholic Church, even as it gave up its temporal powers. One hundred years later, in the middle of the bloodiest and most unbelieving century in history, Pope Pius XII declared the Doctrine of the Assumption, which reaffirmed the importance of two crucial Catholic ideas: the sacredness of the body and legitimacy of praying the Rosary. And in the New Dark Ages of the 21st century, Pope St. John Paul II added the Mysteries of Light to the Rosary, calling the world to conversion, to the Eucharist, and to contemplating the unique role of the Mother of God, mystically connected to Christ from his birth, through his ministry, to his death and resurrection, the one who prompted Christ's first miracle, and who turns to us and says: "Do whatever he tells you."

We need to explain—and more importantly, *demonstrate*—that devotion to Mary does not take anything away from our worship of Christ. On the contrary, it draws us closer in every way. The fullness of our faith should make them want what we have, so that they will repeat what was said after Mary bid her son to perform that first miracle: "You have saved the good wine till now."

Chapter Forty

SECTARIAN AND NON-SECTARIAN

As Catholics, we make a claim that is not always comfortable to make. We claim to be, as we repeat in our Creed, the *One, Holy, Catholic, and Apostolic Church*. We do not claim to be merely a particular brand of Christianity. We do not claim to be another sect. We do not even claim to be a sect. We claim to be *The Church*. Not *a* Church. *The* Church. The Church that Christ Himself founded, building it on a foundation that He nicknamed "the Rock," or Peter, and whom he made the Keeper of the Keys. It is no small claim.

What is a sect? A sect is a section. The Protestant denominations are sects, or sections, of the universal truth. The word "denomination" simply means "name." Each sect has a different name; each is a section that has at some point broken off from the Church, or, in most cases, broken off from a section that broke off from the Church. Being a section does not mean it is necessarily false, but rather incomplete. It is a piece of the truth, but a section can never be as complete as the whole.

What does "sectarian" mean? It has to do with what concerns a sect. But here is where the word "sectarian" is misused. We often hear Catholics referred to as "sectarian," as if our concerns were small or narrow. But our concerns are not narrow. Our concerns are about the souls of our children (when it comes to education). Our concerns are about the souls of our neighbor's children (when it comes to abortion). Our concerns are about the souls of everyone (when it comes to "lifestyles" or "leisure time" or "legislative agendas" or little things like that that bring about damnation). Our concerns are about getting people to heaven. They are not narrow concerns. They are universal. The Catholic Church is universal. It is not sectarian.

The problem is that the word "sectarian" is used—wrongly—simply to mean "religious." Religion, no matter what religion, is always going to be about ultimate truth, but "sectarian" is always going to have the connotation of being narrow and somehow less important than "secular" things. What does "secular" mean? Though "secular" is supposed to imply the wider world, the word is a very unfortunate choice. It means "of the age," which means it is concerned with the thing that is passing away.

What does "non-sectarian" mean? It is a confusing word, a case of the language being turned inside out. Just as sectarian originally referred to a sect and its particular views, "non-sectarian" referred the attempts to combine the sections, to combine their creeds, to combine these narrow views into a broader view. It originally meant what is now referred to as "non-denominational." But now the term "non-sectarian" is used to indicate something else. It is supposed to mean "non-religious." It is an utterly bogus use of the term, but that is how legislators and news reporters and academics use it. The problem is if they said what they really meant, that is, if they used the terms "religious" and "non-religious" it would be patently offensive and provocative. So the inoffensive, but inaccurate terms "sectarian" and "non-sectarian" are used instead.

As for the original use of "non-sectarian" in the sense of "non-denominational," it was fraught with danger from the beginning. There has certainly been a genuine desire on the part of many Protestants to gain a greater knowledge of the

Christian truth than the bit they've been left with as the result of their own particular history. They are trying to recover the "fundamental" faith even while they are purposely trying to avoid the historical Church. They want something larger than their own denomination, and so they become "non-denominational." But they have not expanded their theology at all; they have only attempted to extend their narrow view to others. Chesterton was able to point this out on his visit to America in 1921. He wrote:

> Nine times out of ten a man's broad-mindedness is necessarily the narrowest thing about him. This is not particularly paradoxical; it is, when we come to think of it, quite inevitable. His vision of his own village may really be full of varieties; and even his vision of his own nation may have a rough resemblance to the reality. But his vision of the world is probably smaller than the world. His vision of the universe is certainly much smaller than the universe. Hence he is never so inadequate as when he is universal; he is never so limited as when he generalises. This is the fallacy in many modern attempts at a creedless creed, at something variously described as essential Christianity or undenominational religion or a world faith to embrace all the faiths in the world. It is that every sectarian is more sectarian in his unsectarianism than he is in his sect. The emancipation of a Baptist is a very Baptist emancipation. The charity of a Buddhist is a very Buddhist charity, and very different from Christian charity. When a philosophy embraces everything it generally squeezes everything, and squeezes it out of shape.

The Creed, says Chesterton, is a thing with a definite shape, and the shape cannot be changed. It cannot be cut up or improved or made more fundamental. It is like a key. It will only work if it remains solid and changeless and whole. A section of a key is useless. Several sections of a key still do not serve the function of a key. Nor do several *non*-sections, for that matter. That is why the keeper of the keys has to protect the key's definite and distinct and complete shape. Because the main function of a key is to open the door.

꿈

Chapter Forty-One

ONE FOOLISH WORD

G.K. Chesterton was a Christian for more than 22 years before he became a Catholic. And yet, during those two-plus decades he defended the Catholic Church on just about every point. He even admitted that he was standing at the door ushering other people into the Church without having entered it himself. When he finally did take that final step himself, it was rather shocking news. George Bernard Shaw, who had long made fun of Chesterton's "Roman Catholic hobby," immediately fired off a letter, saying, "Gilbert, this is going too far!" While there were some who thought he never would become Catholic, there were others who thought he already was one. But most people wondered why it took him so long to fully embrace the thing he had long defended. The question is still often asked: What took Chesterton so long to convert? The usual answer is: his wife. And it is not a criticism. He shared a special intimacy with Frances Chesterton, and was very dependent on her. But she was a devout Anglican, and the idea of doing anything independently of her, especially something so vitally important, was almost unthinkable. It was a brave and poignant moment when, in 1922, Chesterton made his decision to become a Catholic... all alone. On the day he was received into the Church, he was happy, and she was happy for him, and yet they both wept. They both knew that suddenly there was something huge that they did not share. The story ends happily, however, as four years later, Frances joined her husband by joining the One, Holy, Catholic, and Apostolic Church.

But there is another reason for Chesterton's long delay in becoming Catholic, and it has nothing to do with his marriage. It is revealed in his book *The Catholic Church and Conversion*. He writes, "For the convert's sake, it should also be remembered that one foolish word from inside does more harm than a hundred thousand foolish words from outside." To put it another way: there is almost nothing that can be said by an enemy of the Church that will prevent the potential convert from becoming a Catholic, but one wrong word from a Catholic can do a great deal of damage.

Chesterton was not simply making a detached observation when he wrote these words. He is speaking from personal experience. How do I know that? Because in my own experience and in the experiences of almost every Catholic convert I know, this is a cold hard fact: it is not the Catholic faith that keeps people away from the Church: it is Catholics.

And now that I am a Catholic, I am concerned that I might forget how easy it is to cause the potential convert to stumble as he is stepping towards Rome.

What are some examples of saying the wrong thing? What is that one foolish word?

The first thing that comes to mind is "shop talk": the latest Vatican politics and chancery gossip. Nothing can be more off-putting to the Protestant who is already wary of these things. Along the same line is the way we might offhandedly or even enthusiastically refer to saints and sacramentals in mixed company. There are simply wrong times to gush about our chance to see the thighbone of St. Seraphim of Abyssinia or the glittery blue Rosary we bought at the Shrine of Our Lady of Forsooth.

This is not merely speaking a different language: we may as well be promoting our favorite Hindu deities.

But though that is the first thing that comes to mind, it is not the worst thing. Sometimes it is not what we say, but the way we say it that makes people run away from the Catholic Church. We may be affirming the Church's teachings, but if we are arrogant or openly insensitive to Protestant sensitivities, we are our own worst enemy. A devout Catholic is often dismissive of sincere Protestant believers. Using the truth as a sledgehammer is not evangelization. Protestants who are considering the Catholic Church take their Christian faith seriously. It is because they take it seriously that they keep digging deeply into it and eventually discover the thrill and beauty and profundity of the ancient Church. When they come upon the startling realization that the ancient Church still exists, they don't need to be told that their own Christian faith is deficient. They need to have the truths that they already embrace to be affirmed and then enlarged. They are longing for the whole Truth. That is why they are attracted to the Catholic Church.

There is another kind of danger. The one foolish word that drives people away from the Church may come from an entirely opposite extreme. The potential convert can run into serious trouble by encountering Catholics who know almost nothing about their own faith and who are ready to compromise on any point, when the convert is ready to sacrifice everything for the sake of even the smallest point. The Church's teachings on the Eucharist, on marriage, on abortion and contraception are utterly clear and are not subject to the whims of public opinion. They are an integral part of the fullness of Truth. If we water down the doctrine to make it more palatable, we are leading people astray... and we are leaving them still hungry and thirsty.

We have to avoid the two opposite problems of a bull-headed

condemnation of everything that is not Catholic and a soft-headed tolerance of everything that is not Catholic, or what Chesterton describes as truth that is pitiless and pity that is untruthful. Truth cannot be preached without charity; charity cannot be substituted for truth.

If one foolish word can keep away giants like G.K. Chesterton, imagine the damage we are doing to the thousands of souls who do not have his same intellectual and spiritual gifts. Scary thought.

Chapter Forty-Two

CONSPIRACY THEORIES

Sometimes the truth can be hard to believe. But the proposed alternatives usually turn out to be even worse. Preposterous even. Two things come to mind. The Kennedy Assassination and the Resurrection.

It was difficult for anyone to believe that a lone crackpot could get off three lucky shots and kill the President of the United States. But the alternative explanations—the conspiracy theories—when carefully considered, are much more far-fetched than the startling truth. The different conspiracy theories have Lee Harvey Oswald working for the CIA, the FBI, the KGB, the MOB, the NRA, or NBC. He's either a participant or a patsy, but never acting alone. Some theories don't even have Oswald in them. Or else he's the good guy who was actually trying to stop the assassination. The second (or third) gunman across the Grassy Knoll has been variously identified as one of the Watergate burglars, one of Castro's cousins, Jack Ruby, and even one of Frank Sinatra's ex-drummers. Really. The conspirators covered their tracks by faking photographs, switching Kennedy's body, killing Oswald, and starting the Vietnam War.

I used to give some credence to the conspiracy theories until I actually examined them carefully. If you take all the critics of the Warren Report and put them together, they do not damage the conclusions of the Warren Report, they merely tear apart each other. At the end of this free-for-all, the only account still standing, and still holding together, is the official version: Oswald acted alone in killing Kennedy. And Ruby acted alone in killing Oswald. Two nut cases who slipped through the cracks of humanity, and through the hands of the Secret Service. As unbelievable, as unlikely as it sounds, it is the only scenario that accurately accounts for everything that happened in Dallas in November, 1963.

One conspiracy buff, Josiah Thompson (a philosophy professor who became a private eye), has called the Kennedy Assassination, "a religious event." Indeed, Dealy Plaza is a place of pilgrimage, the Texas School Book Depository a kind of shrine. But like any religion, it draws a lot of heretics, who deny the difficult truth and set up absurd alternatives.

In the 19th century, that is, nineteen centuries after certain eyewitnesses had turned in their testimonies of another "religious event," a varied group of textual criticism buffs emerged who claimed to have found a way "scientifically" to enhance the original accounts, giving us a more accurate picture of what really happened following the execution of a certain Jewish teacher who had been prone to make extravagant claims about himself. The initial report, the one published and sanctioned by the official institution that was established subsequent to the event itself, was that Jesus of Nazareth rose from the dead and that his claims about his own divinity were in fact, true.

But the textual criticism buffs uncovered a conspiracy. Their evidence revealed the real story, a truth that the Church conspired for centuries to keep from the public. The textual criticism buffs, whose descendants survive in this century as a crew called the "The Jesus Seminar," have taken the eyewitness accounts and, as I've said, scientifically enhanced and analyzed them, and have offered alternative explanations of the event in question. One is that Jesus survived his crucifixion. One is that his disciples stole his body (just like Kennedy's body was switched). Or they just lost track of which tomb he was in. Or the whole thing was just a misunderstanding. Or just a hallucination. Or just a good idea, to keep his legend alive. Or that Jesus never lived at all, but was just a legend to begin with. Or, in one theory, Judas is the good guy, trying to prevent Jesus' self-destructive megalomania. They made a musical out of that version.

All of the "natural" explanations are wilder than the miracle. As Chesterton says, "What do modern men say when apparently confronted with something that cannot, in the cant phrase, be naturally explained? Well, most modern men immediately talk nonsense."

And the form of nonsense that always attracts big numbers is the conspiracy theory. We saw this in the feeding frenzy propelled by that book of nonsense, *The Da Vinci Code*, which trotted out everyone's favorite conspiracy theory: the Roman Catholic Hierarchy is Hiding Something Really Big.

"Whenever we say there is a peril of conspiracy," says Chesterton, "we are always ourselves in a great peril of panic. And whenever we are in a great peril of panic, we are always in a great peril of nonsense. That is the great danger of talking about conspiracy."

The textual criticism buffs can never avoid being conspiracy buffs. There is always something sinister in their alternative explanations. They claim there was a conspiracy to hide the truth, that the people who knew that Jesus was really dead promulgated a lie to make him appear the unlikely victor over his enemies and detractors, one of whom was Death, and that the Catholic Church has continued to participate in the cover-up for its own enrichment, no doubt.

The problem with all the alternative explanations of the

Resurrection is that none of them account for everything that was actually recorded or has happened since. None of them deal honestly with the fact that crucifixion is not something one lives through, that a prominent man offered the use of his own tomb, that the King stationed guards at the tomb to prevent against grave-robbery, that those witnesses who claimed to have seen the risen Jesus had nothing to gain for their testimonies other than mockery, persecution, and martyrdom. And none of them explain how a myth or a misunderstanding or a lie could continue to construct architecture for twenty centuries. Not just churches, mind you, but schools, hospitals, and missions. A vast conspiracy indeed.

None of the other explanations get at the truth. As hard as it is to believe in the Resurrection, the other explanations are simply nonsense. More importantly, the other explanations, the conspiracy theories, are not explanations at all; they are only attacks on the Church. Century after century, the Church has had to deal with its enemies. Not by trying to hide anything, but by throwing open its doors and welcoming everyone in. And yet, as Chesterton says, "Its enemies go on desperately calling it a conspiracy."

There is, however, one interesting note about conspiracies in the case of Jesus: there really *was* a conspiracy to kill him. And it would have succeeded entirely but for one wrinkle: Jesus rose from the dead.

Chapter Forty-Three

THE CULT OF PROGRESS

Whenever you hear the word "progress," a loud alarm should go off inside your head. Someone is trying to slip something by you. Be suspicious. Your immediate response to the word should be to ask the question: "Progress towards what?" There cannot be progress, there cannot be improvement, unless we first identify where we are coming from and where we are going. In order to measure progress, you need to know the starting point and the goal. Then you can determine if you are farther along from the starting point than you were before, and closer to the goal. But there are those who call themselves "progressive" and have never bothered telling us where exactly their progress is taking us. Their starting point seems to be tradition and the truths handed down to us through the centuries. They consider themselves to be making progress the farther they move away from these truths and traditions. They throw out the time-honored forms of worship, the prayers, the music, the art, the architecture, the moral teaching, the ancient wisdom, the faith of our fathers, but they have nothing to offer in its place. Their churches are bare, their art is formless, their prayers are vague, their music is ugly, their teaching is full of doubt. And they don't know where they are going. But they are still convinced they are closer than they were before.

G.K. Chesterton recognized the false Cult of Progress in the early 20th century, the claim that the world is always advancing step by step, though no one will ever say where the next step will be.

> So far from saying that all roads lead to Rome, they lay it down as a fixed infallible dogma that no roads can possibly lead to Rome, even while as loudly asserting that they do not know where any of their own roads lead. Their own roads, by their own description, go winding about with every conceivable or inconceivable new curve or deflection; but they cannot possibly point to the central city of our civilization even when thousands who have traveled on those new roads have actually already arrived at that ancient place.

They always assert that nothing is final, that nothing must be accepted as absolute, but ironically, there are some things they absolutely reject. They reject the past. They accept everything in the future, even though they don't know what it is. Though they call themselves "progressive," there is actually something rather backwards about their philosophy of insisting that our fathers were wrong but our children are right. They will listen to anything, but "they refuse to listen to reason if it requires them to listen to Rome."

As Chesterton points out, the false cult of progress is directly connected to Darwin's theory of evolution. Whatever the merits of the biological evidence to support that theory, the problem is that the theory utterly infected social and religious thought in the 19th century. T.H. Huxley seized on Darwin's ideas in order to justify his own agnosticism, and he was singularly responsible for popularizing Darwinism throughout the world, especially among the other skeptics like himself. The great intellectuals who doubted that God had created the heavens and the earth suddenly put all their faith in the heavens and the earth somehow creating themselves. They weren't sure how it worked and how it all started, but they were quite sure that everything has been constantly getting better and will keep improving. We will evolve higher and higher. Towards what, we do not know. But the practical application of this idea was a strange form of determinism: the idea that whatever happened in the world was simply a necessary step to whatever happened next. It was part of the process, part of the progress. And it was used to justify slave labor, mass starvation, horrendous poverty and even more horrendous wealth. The big will keep on eating the little. Progress.

Chesterton called this idea "a rather curious variation of nature worship, which is not so much the worship of the sun or the worship of the thunder-cloud, but rather the worship of the fog." The progressives cling to the vague mists of the future.

In the 20th century, birth control and then abortion were considered signs of progress. Then euthanasia. Then the normalization of homosexuality. And so on. The supporters of these ideas always refer to them as progress. Towards what?

And what has always been accused of standing in the way of all this progress? The Catholic Church, of course. Yes, the Church has tried to stop poverty and starvation. The Church has slowed the progress of the slaughter of the unborn. The Church has been an obstacle for those misguided souls who would destroy themselves through acting out their perverse desires.

It is the Catholic Church that has always stood for *real* progress. We have a real goal in mind. It is heaven. The works of devotion are designed to help us get to heaven. The works of charity are designed to help others get to heaven. The works of praise and adoration are simply practice for heaven. Real progress is easy to measure. Does it bring us closer to God or not? Does it bring the world closer to God or not?

Chesterton says that sometimes in order to go forward we have to go back, that is, in order to get back on to the right road we have to turn around and return to it. It is called repentance. Repentance is usually the most progressive thing we can do.

Chapter Forty-Four

THE TWO KINDS OF EVIL

G.K. Chesterton once prophetically pointed out that we have achieved the greatest forms of communication in history precisely at the moment when we have nothing to say. There is another irony that he might have observed (and probably did): in spite of our advanced and convenient forms of communication—cell phones, email, instant messaging, etc.—we don't really communicate as well as our predecessors did. Language has decayed. We are increasingly inarticulate. We talk in sound bites, in simplifications. We use catchphrases as substitutes for genuine thinking. We abbreviate everything. In fact, we abbreviate our whole lives. And instead of being drawn closer together by sophisticated forms of communication, we have become increasingly isolated. The camera has become a high-tech mirror, offering distorted pictures of our souls.

In the spring of 2007, we saw a tragic and unimaginable example of this on the campus of Virginia Tech. Various experts and media commentators wrung their hands trying to find an explanation for why a university student would systematically and unemotionally gun down his fellow students. A major news magazine trumpeted this great psychological insight: "Mass killers tend to be aggrieved, hurt, clinically depressed, socially isolated and, above all, paranoid. They believe the world is against them." Well yes, they should be paranoid. The world is, in fact, against mass killers.

Even worse than the useless psychological explanations were the attempts to assign the blame. Somebody else had to be made responsible for failing to treat the mental illness of a disturbed young man. When truth is awful, people often comfort themselves with lies, and getting angry at somebody left standing after the killer lies dead is the best that some bewildered souls can do.

Nothing that I read or heard came close to touching the real solution to this mystery. How does someone descend so deeply into evil, to the point of no return? Chesterton says, "Men may keep a sort of level of good, but no man has ever been able to keep on one level of evil. That road goes down and down." Sin is our own fault; confession is our own responsibility. But if continued, unconfessed sin leads to enslavement. We no longer control it; it controls us. The cold fury of the shooter at Virginia Tech was not merely unnatural, it was supernaturally unnatural. It was demonic.

When Christ began his ministry on earth, he found a world full of demons, that is, a world full of people possessed by demons. He spent a great deal of his time casting them out. In perhaps the most notorious account, he confronted the Gadarene demoniac, wandering wildly among the tombs, naked and mutilating himself. Chains could not hold him. Christ demanded to know the demon's name. "Legion," came the answer, "For we are many." When he commanded the demons to leave the man's body, they begged to be cast into a herd of swine. Christ gave them leave, and they entered the swine, and the pigs stampeded off a cliff to their deaths. When the people of Gadarene came, they found the man "clothed and in his right mind." Were they grateful? No, they wanted Jesus to leave. They were more threatened by an exorcist than by a terrifying demon-possessed man.

Exorcists are banished in the modern world, too. To admit that they have a function would be to admit that demons exist. Our doctors and psychologists and sociologists do not cast out demons. They merely explain them away. But the demons are real even though they are no longer called by their proper name. Nor are they called by their poetic name, Legion, for they are many. And the world, like a herd of swine, is rushing to destroy itself. Unfortunately, as Chesterton says, in our modern version of the event at Gadarene, we have kept the demons and the swine, but we have left out the Redeemer.

Chesterton says that there are two kinds of evil: "There is an accidental kind, that you can't see because it is so close you fall over as you do over a hassock. And there is the other kind of evil, the real kind. And that a man will go to seek however far off it is—down, down, into the lost abyss." (A hassock, by the way, is a footrest. Like an ottoman, I guess, not that anyone knows what an ottoman is, either. In any case, something you trip over.)

Those who died that day at Virginia Tech reflected the two kinds of evil: there were those who died accidentally, by being in the wrong place at the wrong time. And one who died purposefully, seeking the lost abyss.

The horror of it captured our attention. Everyone noticed it and had to find a way to deal with it. But there is a worse horror in this country, much worse. It is a dark, festering, widespread evil that gets scant attention. Most people have found a way to ignore it. It is worse because it happens every day. It is worse because it is systematically aided and abetted. Every day thousands of people pursue an evil down, down into the lost abyss of an abortion clinic. And every day thousands of innocent lives are lost. The demons thrive on this evil, and it is time we cast them out. But we have kept the demons and the swine. We have cast out the Redeemer.

Chapter Forty-Five

THE OLD FEUD BETWEEN SCIENCE AND RELIGION

In the last few years, I have had the occasion to give several talks on science and religion in a variety of settings. For some reason this is a very controversial topic, but not for the reason I would have expected. What can always be found in these very different audiences are a few people who get upset at my apparent lack of respect—or rather my lack of complete religious devotion... to Darwin.

They have something else in common: the predictable inability to talk about Darwin without bringing up Galileo. This is a case where a name has become a catchword, and the catchword, as G.K. Chesterton says, has become a substitute for thinking.

It is assumed that we cannot criticize Darwin because "look what happened to Galileo." For the same reason it is assumed that we can always criticize the Church because "look what happened to Galileo."

The widely-believed story about Galileo is that he valiantly stood up for scientific truth and was horribly persecuted by the narrow-minded Catholic Church that favored superstition to science. Some people even think Galileo was burned at the stake for discovering that the earth went around the sun. And they all know that history vindicated Galileo and therefore religion must forever remain silent in the presence of science.

The facts of the case are a little .more subtle. Galileo's conflict with the Church was actually more of a conflict of personalities than anything else, a conflict exacerbated by the arrogance of Galileo himself and his hatred for certain bishops, including the Pope, whose authority he genuinely wished to undermine. He openly told his students and colleagues that since the Church was wrong about one thing, it could not be trusted about anything else. That one thing was the Geocentric theory. He claimed it was wrong and therefore was evidence that the Church was wrong. In response to Galileo's relentless harassment, the Church authorities called him in and told him basically to put up or shut up, that is, to prove that the earth revolved around the sun or cease all public statements about the Heliocentric theory and about the Church. Galileo actually could not prove it, and he knew he could not prove it. He could only continue to hoist the heliocentric theory as a better explanation of observed evidence than the geocentric theory. The Church took this as an opportunity to silence Galileo, that is, to remove him from a teaching position and to confine him to a comfortable palace (not a prison) where he could continue freely to conduct his research. He subsequently did penance, and died at a ripe old age in full communion with the Church, and is buried in a place of honor in the Church of Santa Croce in Florence.

But Galileo did not defy Church dogma about the solar system for the simple reason that there was no Church dogma about the solar system. Nor was the heliocentric theory Galileo's discovery. It had already been put forth almost *a hundred years earlier* by a Polish astronomer named Nicolaus Copernicus, who happened to be a Catholic cleric who was nearly named a bishop. The Church never persecuted Copernicus. On the contrary, he was honored throughout Europe, including being invited to the Vatican as a guest of the Pope, who subsequently created the Vatican Observatory, which still exists.

Just as the Church does not have any dogma about heliocentric theory, it does not have any dogma about the theory of evolution. However, the Church makes two important pronouncements about the origin of matter and the origin of the human soul, which incidentally are not matters of science, but something quite beyond the reach of science. God created the heavens and the earth. And God created man in His own image. The Church makes no pronouncements about the possible evolutionary pre-history of the universe or of biological development on this particular speck of the universe.

There is one thing, however, that has undergone clear and demonstrable evolutionary change: Darwinism. In light of subsequent discoveries about genetics, even scientists no longer accept "classical" Darwinism. The leading theory at present is that instead of slow, gradual subtle changes in biological development, there were bursts of rapid, complex, and dramatic change to account for the incredible variety of life forms on our mysterious planet. So, it is not because the Church has been wrong about science, but because science has been wrong about science, that the Church plays its cards so close to its vestments in making any statements at all about science.

There are any number of criticisms against Darwinism, especially in how it has been put into practice as a philosophy, but there is presently a hesitation to suggest any weakness in the theory because any criticism of Darwinism is taken to mean that the critic adheres to six-day creationism. At the other extreme, our fundamentalist friends think that any wavering from a literal biblical creationism means one has not only swallowed all of Darwin but also the devil.

As usual, the Church has had to keep its balance, lest it fall into error in one direction or the other. It is important that we insist on the divine origin of the universe and the divine origin of man. There is no compromise on these points. A purely materialist philosophy, applying Darwinism to social theory and public policy and moral behavior, produced some of history's greatest horrors in the scientific age of the 20th century. But whenever I bring these things up, I am predictably rebutted with the atrocities committed in the name of Christianity. This is to precisely miss the point. It is also the opposite argument. Christian misbehavior does not prove that Christianity is wrong. On the contrary, it proves that it is right. Sin is part of our dogma. But eugenics, mass murder, genocide can be directly attributed to people implementing Darwinism as a philosophy.

The point is that evolution, and all scientific theories, can be studied and tested and debated about, but always kept in their place—which is a secondary place. They can never be allowed to touch morality and religion. How can the position of the planets or the diet of the dinosaurs possible matter as to whether we should lie, steal, murder, cheat? As G.K. Chesterton says, "The truth at the back of all the confusion is quite simple. The truth is that the evolutionary theory, if true, is totally useless for human affairs. It is enormous, but irrelevant. Like the solar system, it is a colossal trifle."

※

Chapter Forty-Six

INTELLIGENT DESIGN

A good number of people think "Intelligent Design" deserves more attention, especially in the classroom. They are of the opinion that purely evolutionary explanations do not satisfactorily account for all the complexities seen in biology, from the cellular level to the incredibly intricate combinations that have resulted in wings and eyeballs and brains and other useful mutations like that. Intelligent Design explicitly implies that there is an outside force at work in evolution. "Outside force" of course, suggests a Creator. Some call it God. There's the rub.

Thus, Harvard University has received an ongoing grant of one million dollars a year to *disprove* Intelligent Design. Disprove. One Million Dollars. A year. You read that right.

I do not know where that grant came from, but somebody is evidently threatened by the concept of design in biology, the idea that life is not an unintended byproduct of a pointless process. I guess I should not have used the word "process," because even that implies design. Perhaps it is a flaw of our language, but almost every biological explanation implies design at some point. In spite of the fact that the unvarnished theory of evolution means that life and everything we see and know and are is the random result of a mindless atomic accident, scientists still sound almost mystical when they talk about "Nature" (capital "N"). They refer to Nature's "purpose," its "determination," its "perseverance," its "patterns," its ... well, "design." Really, we should not even say "accident," because to say that something is unintended implies that there is missed intention somewhere.

It is ironic that Catholic thinkers—and Catholic scientists— have never been as threatened by the theory of evolution as certain evolutionists are now threatened by the theory of Intelligent Design. The reason is simple. For Catholics, there is no scientific theory that can ever disprove or damage or even intimidate religious truth. The Truth revealed to the Church is eternal and unchangeable. It is this: God created the heavens and the earth. God created Man in the Image of God. Man was created perfect, but he sinned. The Fall brought a curse upon the entire human race, a curse that was broken by the extraordinary act of God Himself becoming a Man and sacrificing Himself for all of mankind. Whatever mechanistic processes God created are subject to logic and reason and are worthy of study. The mechanics of the created world may involve evolution, including the evolution of life, and the majority of evidence seems to support this idea, however, there may be scientific explanations that come along that better account for the nagging phenomena that the present scientific theories do not account for. This is precisely what the history of science (which grew within the Church) has shown.

For the agnostic or atheistic evolutionist, however, "Intelligent Design" is indeed a threat. A godless explanation of nature is absolutely necessary to provide a foundation for a godless philosophy and a wholly secular society where religion is marginalized.

The *philosophy* of evolution—not the scientific theory—has been used to justify almost all of the worst things the world has seen for the last 150 years. Andrew Carnegie used Darwinism to justify his exploitation of workers. Nietzsche used Darwinism to support his idea of a "superman," which was subsequently seized upon by Hitler to fuel his ideas about a master race. Evolution has been used to reinforce the philosophy of materialism which attacks the doctrine of free will and reduces all human behavior to mere mechanical reactions or biological reflexes. Evolution has been invoked to degrade religion, from publicity stunts like the Scopes Monkey Trial to the dark workings of Eugenics with its wanton destruction of human beings whether in the womb or in the wheelchair.

This, of course, is a misuse of science. Chesterton says that science must never be used to impose a philosophy upon us: "Science cannot tell us what to believe anymore than the telephone can tell us what to say."

Chesterton, like other Catholic thinkers, was completely untroubled by the theory of evolution. But he was also unimpressed with it. He pointed out any number of weaknesses in Darwin's theory, including the rather remarkable lack of key fossil evidence. He wryly observes: "They continue to demonstrate the Darwinian theory from the geological record, by means of all the fossils that ought to be found in it." The gaping holes in the fossil record continue to be as problematic as they have always been, provoking constant revision in the explanations of how more complicated life forms have suddenly appeared. But the missing link is still missing. Chesterton says, "If there were a missing link in a real chain, it would not be called a chain at all."

Chesterton speculates that the Garden of Eden may or may not be an allegory, but in any case the point of the story is this: "Man, whatever else he is, is certainly not merely one of the plants of the garden or one of the animals of the garden. He is something else, something strange and solitary."

The strangest thing that this strange and solitary creature should do is theorize that he is himself merely an animal that happens to be sitting on top of the evolutionary heap. Perhaps the most damaging idea that has come from the philosophy of evolution is the notion of endless progress, that the world and mankind just keep getting better. The bloodshed of the 20th century, the most massive violent extermination of human life in all of history, seems to contradict the idea of "progress." Our knowledge of the natural world has certainly increased greatly through the centuries. Our knowledge of the human soul, however, is the same as what it was 2000 years ago: we are sinful creatures in need of redemption.

There is too much that the purely "natural" explanations simply do not explain. For instance, our appreciation of beauty. The fact that we recognize beauty suggests that the beauty of the world is not a work of nature, but a work of art. And if it is a work of art, says Chesterton, "then it involves an artist." It is a basic sense of appreciation, of gratitude, that points to something larger than ourselves, larger than the world, even larger than the universe. And so, says Chesterton, "What we call Nature, the wiser of us call Creation."

Chesterton seems to predict that Intelligent Design would someday become an issue in the questions about the origin and development of life: "Evolution as an explanation... of the cause of living things, is still faced with the problem of producing rabbits out of an empty hat; a process commonly involving some hint of design."

Perhaps the objection from the folks at Harvard is not to the idea of "design," but to the idea of "intelligent." Perhaps they are not satisfied with the design. Perhaps they think they could have done a better job themselves at creating the universe. In which case their sin is that of Lucifer's, who thought he was better suited to be God.

ॐ

Chapter Forty-Seven

CLONING AND OTHER EVILS

If talented men were mated with talented women, of the same
mental and physical characters as themselves...we might
produce a highly bred human race...If we divided the rising
generation into two castes, A and B, of which A was selected
for natural gifts, and B was the refuse, then supposing marriage
was confined within the pale of [each] caste...we should then...
hasten the marriages in caste A, and retard those in caste B...
and would end by wholly eliminating B, and replacing it by
A... The law of natural selection would powerfully assist...by
pressing heavily on the minority of weakly and incapable men.

Thus wrote Francis Galton in 1865, a mere six years after the
publication of Charles Darwin's *Origin of the Species.* Inspired by
Darwin's theory of evolution, Galton developed the idea of the
controlled breeding of humans, and called it "Eugenics." Darwin
called Galton's ideas "admirable." I suppose it makes sense that
the two of them had such praise for one another and such a
high opinion of proper heredity. They were, after all, cousins.

Francis Galton proposed Eugenics "for the betterment of
mankind," since only the best and the brightest would be involved in the business of making babies. Although the idea
sounds absurd and inhuman, it was enthusiastically embraced
over the next generation by leading scientists (such as botanist
Luther Burbank), leading intellectuals (such as George Bernard
Shaw), and leading newspapers (such as the *New York Times*).

The two most famous advocates of Eugenics were Margaret Sanger, the founder of Planned Parenthood, and Adolph Hitler, the founder of Planned Genocide. The latter, some would admit, gave Eugenics a bad name. But unfortunately he made the word disappear, and lost in all that commotion was the fact that the feminist icon who ushered in the wide acceptance of birth control in the 20th century was a racist who advocated "more children for the fit, less for the unfit."

At the height of its popularity, there was only one notable writer who wrote a book *against* Eugenics: G.K. Chesterton. He saw through its vacant promises and predicted that the same mentality that embraced Eugenics would endorse birth control and then abortion and then infanticide. Chesterton's book *Eugenics and Other Evils* is an astounding read. Sort of like everything else he wrote. One of the astounding things about this book is that if you took the word "Eugenics" and replaced it with the word "cloning," you would marvel at how Chesterton cuts right to the heart of the matter in the present debate over this latest scientific controversy.

All of the arguments in favor of eugenics could also be used in favor of cloning. It is for "the betterment of mankind." It would help fight disease. It would alleviate great suffering. And besides, you can't stop progress. Bow-wow woof-woof.

But cloning, like eugenics and like abortion, bases all its benefits on denying an entire class of humans their humanity. With eugenics it was the "unfit," which usually meant the poor, the weak, or simply the ethnic-types who were just having too many children for other people's taste. With abortion, it is the weakest and most defenseless humans of all: the unborn. But research cloning goes beyond even that. It is human life deliberately created in order that it will be destroyed, created solely in order that selected tissue might be "harvested" and the rest discarded. As Chesterton warns with chilling accuracy: "They seek his life in order to take it away."

Cloning—like Eugenics—is about the tyranny of the elite deciding who shall live and who shall die. And if it's about the elite, it's about money. It is not only supported by the super-wealthy, it is a potential source of wealth. It was the Rockefellers and the Carnegies and other capitalist lords who funded eugenics research in the early 20th century. They went on to be major supporters of Planned Parenthood. Social science has a Darwinian quality to it, not only in its philosophy, but in its very existence: only the social scientists with the most funding survive. They are funded by rich philanthropists. And as Chesterton prophesies, they try inhuman experiments, and when they fail, they try even more inhuman experiments. They are inhuman because they are godless. But they are godless because they don't want to face how inhuman they are. The wealthy industrialist became agnostic, says Chesterton, "not so much because he did not know where he was, as because he wanted to forget. Many of the rich took to skepticism exactly as the poor took to drink; because it was a way out."

The advocates of cloning research will tell you it is about health and saving lives. It is not. It is about money. All of the cloning research at Texas A & M has been funded by a corporation in California that has invested in marketing a pet-cloning service.

And even though it is clearly not about health and saving lives (because it is not about saving the lives that would be created and discarded), the argument about health is still misplaced. As Chesterton says, our modern worship of health is unhealthy. "The cult of hygiene today is not so much materialistic as mystical. Health is preferred to life; and the experts seem to be more satisfied with a well-nourished corpse than with a lively cripple."

We have utterly lost the meaning of suffering, the ancient lesson of the book of Job. And that is because we have lost the meaning of life.

The advocates of cloning do not say what is the real purpose of cloning. They don't say because they're not sure themselves. They haven't thought it out clearly. They don't understand the evil that lies beneath it.

Chesterton says, "Evil always takes advantage of ambiguity... Evil always wins through the strength of its splendid dupes; and there has in all ages been a disastrous alliance between abnormal innocence and abnormal sin." He says that all the newspapers and public speakers are always trying to find harmless words for a horrible thing. This is the *Age of Euphemism*. We talk of Birth Control when we mean no birth and no control. We talk of tissue when we mean an unborn baby. We talk of Abortion when we mean the slaughter of babies. We talk of Eugenics, when we mean the extermination of an entire race. Chesterton says it is a weak and washy sort of idealism, presented as a kind of humanitarianism, but it is a sheer stark inhumanitarianism. It is inhuman. It is horrible.

We have lost the meaning of life. It has been turned into merely the struggle for existence. This meaninglessness, this purposelessness, is seen in many of our other scientific pursuits. It is perhaps epitomized in the space program. No one can say what the purpose of space exploration is. G.K. Chesterton said something pretty interesting about it in 1917. He said, "leaving the earth would be of no earthly use, and empty space would be literally vanity." In the wake of each of the space shuttle tragedies, almost the first thing out of the mouths of government officials was that the space program would continue. What they do not explain is why. What they did not explain was the purpose of all these very expensive trips to nowhere and back. Now that the space shuttle program has been shelved, we continue "unmanned" exploration (that still has to be paid for by man) to lifeless planets looking for evidence of life, while we ignore or destroy life here at home.

Chesterton says the problem with official science is that it steadily becomes more official while it becomes less scientific. "The man in the street," he says, "must be wholly at the mercy of an academic priesthood." If people who care about traditional truths attempt to object to eugenics or birth control or cloning, they are barraged with what Chesterton calls "the same stuffy science, the same bullying bureaucracy, and the same terrorism by tenth-rate professors."

"Science," says Chesterton, "is a vast design for producing accidents." Some of these accidents are quite spectacular. Eugenics blew up. Space exploration blew up. Atomic energy blew up and will blow up again. We cannot even imagine what horrible accidents could result from these experiments in human cloning, although Hollywood has imagined some vividly horrible scenarios. The only difference is, this would be real, and we're not ready for it.

G.K. Chesterton was completely right about why Eugenics was completely wrong. As with all of Chesterton's prophetic writing, we could have avoided some terrible problems if we had heeded his warnings. But even now it's not too late. His words still ring true today. Over one hundred years ago, at the dawn of the 20th century, he said, "We are learning to do a great many clever things. The next thing we are going to have to learn is not to do them."

Chapter Forty-Eight

LIFE AND OTHER TRADEOFFS

"Would you trade ten years of your life to know the meaning of life itself?"

In one of those discussions that goes late into the night, I once talked with a famous physician about some of life's most profound mysteries. He said that he often puts that question—that proposition—to his patients and to other doctors: "Would you give up ten years of your life for all the answers to all the questions?"

In every case, he claims, the response is "No." His conclusion from this is that it is more important to search for the truth than actually to know the truth. The search for the truth gives more meaning to people's lives than finding the truth.

This man is a fine doctor, one of the most widely respected in his field, and a truly compassionate healer, justly admired for his excellent bedside manner. But I wondered if his question was unfairly finessed to produce such consistent answers. I knew that he was an agnostic, and I wondered if he was simply trying to reinforce his faith in agnosticism, that is, to maintain a blissful ignorance.

I told him that first of all, there was a problem with his question, and even so, he still misunderstood the answers he had been given.

It is simply unreasonable to conclude that we are more

content asking ultimate questions than having them answered, unless of course, we are purposely avoiding and evading the answer, *because we know the answer.* Obviously it is more soothing to go on asking questions rather than being troubled by facing the answer, especially if the answer requires us to change our lives, maybe even to stop sinning.

This doctor said he really believed that people are not only more content with the search for truth than the discovery of it, but that they are better served by the search than by the discovery. This is a sadly cynical conclusion to which to resign oneself: that the truth is not worth knowing but that the dance around it is good for a few laughs.

But you sometimes get the wrong answer, because you have asked the wrong question.

His question to his patients is not a real question. It is not a real tradeoff. Such a choice is simply not possible: ten years or truth. There is no one to grant either one or the other. The answers are revealing, but they do not reveal what the doctor thought they did. The answers reveal that life is precious. Every normal person hesitates to give up life; generally we would only be willing to give up life as an act of sacrifice. His proposition, however, would not be a sacrifice; it would be more like a deal with the devil, because we would be bargaining with sacred goods for our own nebulous gratification.

A more fruitful question would be: would you give up ten years of your life to save someone else's life? I would imagine the answer to that question would much more often be "Yes." And that answer better reveals the truth alluded to in the first proposition. Part of the ultimate meaning of life *is* sacrifice. Any sacrifice we make points to the ultimate sacrifice made by God Himself. We embrace this truth as an act of faith, and it gives meaning to all of life and eternity. If we reject this truth, then we must content ourselves with questions rather than answers, for there is no other answer that will be satisfying.

This doctor also told me about some of the truly amazing breakthroughs in medical technology, astonishing stories of patients being successfully treated for blindness, deafness, paralysis, Parkinson's Disease, Alzheimer's Disease. Some of these experimental treatments have involved the use of stem cells. Interestingly enough, he said that stem cells have had no role in the treatment or even potential treatment of Parkinson's or Alzheimer's (directly contrary to the claims by the advocates of stem cell research), however, there do seem to be some genuine possibilities using stem cells for the treatment of spinal cord injuries. He stressed, however, that these results are very preliminary and have not been achieved in humans but in animals. I asked him if these experiments were being conducted with embryonic stem cells or adult stem cells. He said the experiments were being done with both.

This raises a new question that might be asked to patients and doctors: "Would you sacrifice a baby so that you could walk again?" Because that could, indeed, be the trade-off. It is not hypothetical. It is a very real possibility.

But that is a question that is not being asked.

Chapter Forty-Nine

THE EARTH AND OTHER HOT TOPICS

There are two rather wrong and simplistic attitudes toward the environment. One position is that humans are the enemy of the natural world, something like alien life forms that are rapidly destroying the earth, eating it up and heating it up and leaving nothing but barren, baked lake bottom. We have raped and ravaged poor old Mother Nature. The other attitude is that there is plenty of earth to be had, a bountiful cornucopia, and anybody who worries about the water, the whales, the oat bran or the ozone is a Chicken Little. And Mother Nature is a big girl who can take care of herself.

The problem comes down to one simple issue, which, as you probably supposed, Chesterton explains better than anyone else. It is this: Nature is not our Mother. Nature is our Sister, for we both have the same Father. This is how we must address the cant on both sides of the environmental debate. We treat our sister with respect, of course. We do not abuse her. We protect her. But we do not worship her. Nature is not a goddess, which is exactly how many environmentalists regard her. But she is a fellow creature, which the other side tends to forget. For both reasons, this is why Chesterton says: What some of us call Nature, the wiser of us call Creation. By looking at the environment as creation, we remember the Creator, which is always the wisest thing we can do.

The term "environmentalist" is one of those large, urgent-sounding words that is actually quite devoid of real meaning. The word environment simply means one's surroundings, the place in which one lives. We can, I suppose, be devoted to our surroundings to some degree, devoted to our home, to our garden, to our field and to the nearby forest. But these are secondary things. We cannot be an "-ist" about them. We cannot be devoted to them with the same devotion as that of a religion, which is about ultimate things. Our devotion is misplaced if it is about the place in which we live and not about life itself, which is the supreme achievement of Creation, especially the lives of those who have been created in the image of the Creator. One of the oddest holes in the environmentalist arguments in defense of nature is the utter lack of respect for human life, especially that of the unborn. And ironically, lovers of nature often take a very unnatural view of sex, the natural purpose of which is to procreate.

But when environmentalists, for lack of a better term, warn about the dangers from excessive pollution and a total disregard for the earth, their misdirected devotion that may make them crazy does not necessarily make them liars. The pollution is still real. The arguments may not be clear, but neither is the air and water, which lends their cloudy arguments some weight.

Pollution and litter and waste as well as wasteful consumption are not merely disrespectful of nature; they are disrespectful of our neighbor. The commandment that we should love our neighbor as ourselves applies to almost everything we do, including the way we use things up and the way we throw things away. Keeping the environment clean, as a way of loving our neighbor as ourselves is an idea that is somehow lost on too many of us. For instance, my son's room looks like a giant wastebasket. Interestingly enough so does my daughter's. They need to grasp the second part of the equation before they can understand the first part. Self-respect begins with picking up your dirty clothes. Loving your neighbor as yourself is sure to follow.

Making our messes someone else's problem is not a way of loving our neighbor. But claiming that our messes are not even a problem at all is simply a lie, which damages us as much as our neighbor.

Psalm 24 begins: "The earth is the Lord's and the fullness thereof, the world and those who dwell therein; for he has founded it upon the seas and established it upon the rivers." We all belong to God. The world he has given us, and all its fullness, is a gift. It is something we do not deserve. Our proper attitude toward this gift is to treat it as something precious, worthy of its Creator. Our throwaway mentality diminishes our appreciation of things. Simply by having the attitude of thankfulness, we are inspired to take better care of things. And the Psalmist says, interestingly enough, that the earth is founded upon the waters. The image is significant. Water is basic. It soothes, it cleans, it refreshes. It must be clean. It must be pure. The Psalmist goes on to wonder how we may approach the hill of the Lord. "Who shall stand in his holy place?" Who? The one who is clean. We praise God "with clean hands and a pure heart." A clean body and clean conscience. But we do not "lift up our soul to what is false." That is, we don't worship the earth, we don't worship the environment. We take care of it, we enjoy it, we give God thanks for it. But we worship the Creator not the creation.

Chapter Fifty

THE STATE OF THE SCHOOLS

I recently had a conversation with a fine fourteen-year-old fellow, sweet-spirited and intellectually hungry, who is presently attending a public school. We were talking about art and literature, and I asked him what his class was studying.

He very excitedly told me they were reading a book about Buddha.

"*Siddhartha* by Herman Hesse?" I asked.

"Yes! It's great!"

"And why is it great?"

"Because it explains how cool Buddha was. And his philosophy."

"And what was his philosophy?"

"It's about achieving Nirvana."

"And how do you explain Nirvana?"

"It's a state of peace, where we have no desires."

"So we achieve perfect peace by suppressing all desire? Do you realize that is precisely the opposite of Catholic philosophy? The same way, I suppose, that the East is the opposite of the West."

He gave me a puzzled look, mixed with a twinge of distaste, since I had brought religion into a conversation about literature— and obviously you can't mix up religion with education.

"What do you mean?" he asked.

"The Catholic Church teaches that our ultimate goal is perfect communion with God, that God is the fulfillment of our deepest desire. Do you see the difference between a philosophy that teaches fulfillment by the suppression of desire and one that teaches the fulfillment of desire by the one eternal being that can fulfill it?"

He admitted he could see the distinction.

"And which gives meaning to the word 'hope'?"

"Well, if you put it that way: Christianity."

"Yes, that is because hope is a purely Christian virtue, like faith and love. You can't really say that Buddhism has hope, since it desires not fulfillment but simply desires to do away with desire."

He knew he was in forbidden territory, so he started looking for a way out. "But you agree," he said, "that the greatest virtue is tolerance, and that the worst thing is intolerance."

"Well, how far does this tolerance thing go? Should I be tolerant of people who torture children? Should I be tolerant of men who rape women?"

His expression explained that he hadn't thought about that. "But how do you know you're right?"

"There really are only two choices," I explained. "There is the East and the West. The East is Buddhism, which leads to Nirvana. Nothingness. It is essentially Atheism. But the West is not just Theism. It is the Incarnation. It is God becoming flesh, becoming a man so that we can know God, so that we can overcome the separation we have from God, which is what sin is: separation from God. The West is epitomized by the Catholic Church, which built our Civilization. Everything else is in the West is some variation of Catholic theology or some reduction of it. So the choice is ultimately between East and West. I choose the West. How do I know I'm right? Well, for one thing, I think my faith can be defended reasonably."

This brought a sudden shift in our conversation to the subject of science and about what can actually be known. He argued that in science you can really prove things, and in religion you can't. I argued that all truth has to serve an ultimate truth, so even the so-called "practical" sciences (e.g. studying geology in order to find oil) are meaningless unless there is a grand purpose to our existence.

But when I brought up meaning, he brought up the subject of art. He told me that the other things he was studying at his school were Picasso and Jazz and Rock music.

Now, I suppose I could vent my wrath against the public schools because they claim they do not allow religion to be taught, and yet they sneak Buddhism into a literature class or materialism into a science class, but it was the subject of art that was actually the most revealing part of the discussion and most epitomized what is wrong with modern public education.

These students were being taught to appreciate Picasso because Picasso is "revolutionary" and "misunderstood," but in the meantime they have never heard of Picasso's predecessors, painters such as Leighton, Bouguereau, or Alma-Tadema. They study Jazz and Rock because this music is "innovative" and "revolutionary," but they have no exposure to Dvorak or Mendelssohn, much less Bach and Mozart. Or Hildegard von Bingen.

In other words, they are studying reactionary art, but they do not know what is being reacted against. The latent assumption is that what is old is bad, the unspoken logic is the older the worse, and the silent conclusion is that art was stilted and stale and held captive by the Catholic Church until the modern world continually freed it. But this is only implied. They don't actually study Gothic architecture or stained glass or Giotto or Fra Angelico. Too old and irrelevant.

The irony is that Picasso is now old, and even passé. Cubism kind of square. Even rock music has gotten creaky. And these revolutionaries were not exactly martyrs. They got rich and comfortable, and even the rebellion became just an act. It is hard to imagine that their goal was to make it into a high school textbook. Yet they are still being treated as if they are new and revolutionary.

G.K. Chesterton says that he can trust the uneducated, but not the badly educated. We have a very badly educated public because the official schools are handcuffed in what they can teach. They have to substitute a shallow philosophy for a deep one, or a subtly Eastern philosophy for an overtly Western one.

One of the main reasons I helped start Chesterton Academy is that I could not afford to wait around for someone else to fix the sorry state of public education—or for it to fix itself. The problem is not just the way it has been infected by a decadent popular culture; the problem is the content of the classes that are actually being taught and the way it is being taught. Unfortunately, most private schools, even religious schools, simply ape the public model. Students are taught skepticism instead of faith, reactionary ideas instead of fundamental ones, modern art and literature instead of the classics, fragmented topics instead of the whole truth. They are not being taught to think, but rather to spew out a few catchphrases about tolerance and innovation. And they are being to taught to dance deliberately around the Catholic Church, either trying to ignore it or to give it an occasional kick.

ॐ

Chapter Fifty-One

THE GOSPEL OF HOSPITALITY

Pope Benedict's first encyclical, "God is Love," beautifully reflects the *first* Pope's first encyclical. You will be surprised to know that you probably have a copy of that ancient document. It is in your New Testament. It is the First Epistle of St. Peter. In it, the first Pope writes "Above all hold unfailingly your love for one another, since love covers a multitude of sins." (I Peter 4:8) The next verse tells exactly how we can translate this ideal called love into action: "Practice hospitality ungrudgingly to one another."

When I have traveled around the country and around the world, I have been blessed many times by people practicing the Gospel of Hospitality. But on one particular trip I experienced it in an especially profound way in two very different but surprisingly connected places. The first was a Benedictine monastery. Clear Creek Monastery is set in the foothills of the Ozarks in eastern Oklahoma. It is relatively new but very devoted to the traditional Benedictine monastic idea of work and prayer. The monks pray the office seven times a day, chanting in Latin. When I was there, they were in a temporary enclosure that they built with their own hands, but they were in the process of building a permanent Romanesque church and enclosure designed to last as long as the grand monasteries of Europe that have been standing for over a thousand years.

I had the privilege of being invited into their chapter house to give a talk on my favorite writer and also to dine with them in a simple and hearty meal. A monk waited on me with more attention than I have ever received in a fine restaurant, washing my hands for me, serving the food and clearing the plates. All done in silence, while another monk, in a chant-like tone, read some spiritual writings. The Rule of St. Benedict calls for every guest to be treated like Christ. Nothing will make you feel more unworthy. Believe me.

The second place at which I stayed made me feel even more unworthy, if that is possible. I was an honorary homeless person at the Casa Juan Diego, a Catholic Worker house in Houston, Texas. It is run by a saintly couple, Mark and Louise Zwick, faithfully adhering to the vision of the original Catholic Worker houses founded by Dorothy Day over a half century ago. Everyone who comes to them is treated like an honored guest. Like *the* honored guest. Like Christ.

The Zwicks, like Dorothy Day before them, and like the monks at Clear Creek Monastery, practice the corporal works of mercy which comprise the Gospel of Hospitality as plainly set forth in Matthew 25:34-40:

> Then the King will say to those at his right hand, "Come, O blessed of my Father, inherit the kingdom prepared for you... for I was hungry and you gave me food, I was thirsty and you gave me drink, I was a stranger and you welcomed me, I was naked and you clothed me, I was sick and you visited me, I was in prison, and you came to me." Then the righteous will answer him, "Lord when did we see the hungry and feed thee, or thirsty and give thee drink? And when did we see thee a stranger and welcome thee, or naked and clothe thee? And when did we see thee sick or in prison and visit thee?" And

the King will answer them, "Truly I say to you, as you did to one of the least of these my brethren, you did it me."

Interestingly, both the monastery and the Catholic Worker house have a Benedictine connection. Dorothy Day was a Third Order Benedictine, and tried as much as possible to apply the rule of St. Benedict to the way that Catholic Worker houses were run. If some modern Catholic Worker houses have not lived up to this ideal, the Houston Catholic Worker house certainly has. Dorothy Day was also very devoted to the writings of G.K. Chesterton, who defended human dignity against all of the modern forces that devalue humans—especially in large urban areas. Mark and Louise Zwick welcome their guests and assist them in any way they can but the idea is always to help them become self-sufficient, because this will give them back their dignity. They help people get on their feet. In some cases, literally. One poor fellow had fallen under a train and lost his foot. He was an "undocumented worker," which means he had nowhere to go for help. Mark arranged for him to get a prosthetic foot. He told me, "You have no idea what it is like to see someone come hobbling in on one leg, and then being able to walk away on two legs."

I have heard from some people who sneer at the work the Zwicks are doing because they help undocumented workers. Ironically, most of the people are brought to them by the Immigration and Naturalization Service or by the police or by the FBI. They are sick, injured, hungry, homeless, helpless. The Zwicks welcome them as they would welcome Christ. These are people who want a better life and have risked everything to get it. It is easy to complain about them from our comfortable chairs next to our full refrigerators. I would meekly suggest that before we complain, we read I Peter 4:9 again: "Practice hospitality ungrudgingly." I would also recommend spending the night in a homeless shelter as I did. Or maybe just spend a night out on the street.

But I have also heard an almost opposite complaint: that the Catholic Worker house is doing the real work of the Church and the monastery is not, that the Catholic Worker house is more relevant and practical and effective than the contemplative monks.

It seems enough to answer that the Benedictines have maintained their way of doing things for well over a thousand years. One does not hang around that long without doing something right. Effective, even.

In medieval times, the monasteries were the center of culture. Wherever a monastery was built a town grew up around it. The monks provided the focus of faith, which always has practical implications that are seen in art, craftsmanship, education, and simple economic stability. It is happening again. Catholic families have already started to settle around the edge of Clear Creek Monastery. This is where they want to raise their children. It is the medieval model working perfectly. They are doing things right, right from the start. Celibate men are planting the seeds in which a culture of families may thrive, which is why Chesterton predicted: "Whenever monks come back, marriages will come back."

The Houston Catholic Worker house also does things right, but in a place where everything has gone wrong, because it went wrong almost from the start. The Zwicks are dealing with one soul at a time in a place where people are cold statistics. Their hospitality cannot solve the large problems that plague huge cities, but it can treat each of the problems that show up at their door everyday. Their source of strength and love is their faith. Each house has a chapel. Jesus is always present, both in the souls of the poor and in the Blessed Sacrament.

I know. I was there.

Chapter Fifty-Two

THE PARADOXICAL SEASON

Lent would seem to be ripe fruit for G.K. Chesterton, the Prince of Paradox. Why? Because it is the most paradoxical of the Christian seasons: a time of both suffering and singing, a time of self-denial and generosity, a time of repentance, that most unpleasant of things that makes us face our sins, and a time of renewal, that most welcome of things, a chance to start over. Starting over is itself a paradox. It means what's done is not done. It means there is life after death.

The word "Lent" means Spring. That's another paradox. Spring, with its renewal and rebirth is just the last thing we associate with Lent.

But even though the paradoxical season seems to beg for Chesterton's commentary, the most surprising paradox is that the man who wrote about everything never wrote about Lent.

And yet he manages to say something about it anyway. He writes about repentance and about the three elements of Lent: Abstinence (or fasting), Charity (or almsgiving) and Prayer. And as we would expect, he sheds light on these subjects.

The Sacrament of Penance, says Chesterton, gives new life and reconciles a man not only to God but to all the living. Being reconciled to each other is how we can achieve a peaceful society. And that is why Chesterton says, "Any Catholic society must have an atmosphere of penance."

In a society that refuses to confess its sins, the idea of forgiveness is strange. We are unable to grasp the concept of starting over. It is because starting over means embracing tradition. It means going back instead of going forward—a rather revolutionary concept.

> There is one metaphor of which the moderns are very fond; they are always saying, "You can't put the clock back." The simple and obvious answer is "You can." A clock, being a piece of human construction, can be restored by the human finger to any figure or hour. In the same way society, being a piece of human construction, can be reconstructed upon any plan that has ever existed. There is another proverb, "As you have made your bed, so you must lie on it"; which again is simply a lie. If I have made my bed uncomfortable, please God I will make it again.

Going back and starting over is what repentance is all about. Repentance means admitting that we have gotten off course and have to go back and start over. "The point of all repentance," says Chesterton, "is beginning afresh."

When asked to define the soul, Chesterton said that a soul is "something that can sin and can sacrifice itself." When we sin, we show how evil we can be. When we sacrifice, we show how good we can be.

The three elements of Lent—sacrifice, charity and prayer—are common themes of Chesterton's. We may not associate a 300-pound, cigar-smoking journalist with fasting and self-control, but he did understand (and practice) the deeper idea of sacrifice: giving up something because it is good, not because it is bad; giving up something not because it helps God, but helps us. He practiced abstinence in ways no one knew. Abstinence and fasting are connected to the idea of sacrifice. The modern world does not understand sacrifice. Chesterton says, "Men often talk of self-sacrifice as if it meant the same as self-subordination or self-effacement. To sacrifice a thing is the Latin for making a thing holy. If you sacrifice yourself you make yourself something solemn and important. The old Pagan did not sacrifice his worst beast; he sacrificed his best beast to his gods." And in the ancient ritual of sacrifice, Chesterton points out that "the gesture of surrender that is most magnificent" is the idea that the man will be the better for losing the ox than that the god will be the better for getting it.

And then there is charity. Chesterton says that charity to the deserving is not charity at all. It is the undeserving who require charity, not the deserving. Chesterton never had any money in his pockets at the end of the day because he gave away whatever he did not spend. He said he knew perfectly well all the arguments against giving money to beggars. But he found them to be precisely the arguments *for* giving money to them. "If beggars are lazy or deceptive or wanting a drink, I know only too well my own lack of motivation, my own dishonesty, my own thirst … I don't believe in 'scientific charity' because that is too easy, as easy as writing a check. I believe in 'promiscuous charity' because that is really difficult. It means the most dark and terrible of all human actions—talking to a man. In fact, I know of nothing more difficult than really talking to the poor men we meet."

Christianity teaches us to feed the hungry and clothe the naked and give shelter to the homeless. And Chesterton takes this even farther. He says this applies to spiritual poverty as well as physical poverty. "As we should be genuinely sorry for tramps and paupers who are materially homeless, so we should be sorry for those who are morally homeless, and who suffer a philosophical starvation as deadly as physical starvation."

And finally, prayer. Prayer is three things: an act of penance, and an act of praise and an act of petition. If we keep these three things in mind, we should be able to fulfill the Apostle Paul's command in I Thessalonians 5:17 to "pray without ceasing." Penance keeps us aware that we are sinners in need of God's mercy and grace. Praise keeps us aware of God's greatness and goodness. And then there is petition. What does petition mean? It means that our prayers really do make a difference.

Chesterton emphasizes that our prayers do make a difference to God; they really do affect God. It means that not everything is stuck in a pre-programmed predestination, but that God can act with reference to our action. This, says Chesterton, "is a great thundering dogma." It is not that we change the mind of God, but that there are certain things that God will not do, certain gifts he will not give, unless we ask him. That is the meaning of Christ's command: "Ask, and you will receive."

Prayer, like fasting and almsgiving is an act of Humility. Not praying is an act of pride. And Chesterton says that pride is the ultimate human evil. "Pride does not go before a fall. Pride is a fall." Which brings us back to prayer as an act of praise and thanksgiving.

Chesterton says that he is astonished at the lack of astonishment we have for creation, for the gift of life. He suggests that we should always be praying the prayer of astonishment, the pious and compact prayer of the first frog: "Lord, how you made me jump!" Reflect on that a while. It is the prayer of surprise. Of astonishment. It is the mystical idea of desiring the very thing we were made for.

In that paradoxical season of Lent, the idea that should inform our abstinence and almsgiving and prayer is thankfulness. We should be thankful for what we are giving up, for what we are giving to others, and for what God has given us to give to others.

It is helpful to look to Chesterton's depth of gratitude, which is unmatched in any other modern writer. He sees our dependence on God in everything. He makes a wonderful reference to St. Peter being crucified upside down. "I've often fancied his humility was rewarded by seeing in death the beautiful vision of ... the landscape as it really is: with the stars like flowers, and the clouds like hills, and all men hanging on the mercy of God." It is an everlasting mercy that we don't fall off.

Chapter Fifty-Three

THE CONTROVERSIES OF CHRISTMAS

We should not be surprised that the word "Christmas" is controversial. As G.K. Chesterton points out, the two syllables that form "Christmas" are two words that have done more to tear the world apart than any other words. Christ and Mass.

The doctrine of the Incarnation has been the biggest source of ongoing theological debate for the past two thousand years. As I pointed out earlier, every major heresy is connected to the person of Christ. The Catholic Church teaches that Christ is fully God and fully Man. Most of the early heresies affirmed the divinity of Christ but denied his humanity. They thought God was too great and good to become flesh, to suffer and die as a man would. They believed that he only appeared to be a man, and consequently only appeared to suffer. But as time passed, the heretics tended to go to the opposite extreme. Christ was considered human but had no more divinity than anyone else; his suffering was only the evidence of his failure as a god. In each case, it was the Catholic Church that held the line, while it was violently accused of imposing either too much divinity or too much humanity onto that mysterious figure called Christ. The main point of Christmas is the Incarnation. It is a doctrine that is affirmed in the very gifts of the Wise Men to the Christ: gold, so that he would be crowned as a king; frankincense, so that he would be worshipped as a God; myrrh, so that he would be buried as a man.

But the Incarnation is only half of the Christmas controversy. In the tragic break up of Christianity, the Protestant reformers wanted to do away with the Catholic Church, which meant, among other things, doing away with the priesthood and the Mass. And, by logical extension, doing away with Christ's Mass: Christmas.

When we say "Merry Christmas" we are affirming a creed that sets Christianity apart from all other religions, but we are also affirming a sacrament that sets the Catholic Church apart from other Christian denominations. We are celebrating Christ's Mass.

While the Christmas controversy began when Christians veered away from the authority of the Church and did not accept the doctrine of Christ and the sacrifice of the Mass, it has continued to our present state of affairs when non-Christians obviously do not accept either of these things. So of course it is controversial to say "Merry Christmas." When we say it, we are saying first that God himself became flesh and blood. We are saying secondly that bread and wine become flesh and blood. There are people who don't believe that. But we do. And nothing should stop us from proclaiming it and celebrating it, because it is indeed tidings of comfort and joy. God has saved us from our sins.

But the controversy does not end there. Let us also understand that everything else about Christmas goes against the culture of death in which we live, even though that culture borrows heavily from the Catholic Church in general and Christmas in particular in order to make its year-end sales quota.

When we sing and recite, "For unto us a child is born," we are wildly rejoicing about the birth of a child in a society that kills millions of babies before they are born.

The controversy goes even deeper. When we proclaim the Virgin Birth we are completely going against a society that preaches contraception. These are direct opposites. The one, says Chesterton, is love without lust. The other is lust without love. In an over-sexed society, two things are hated: virginity and birth. The Christmas miracle goes against the grain in every way. Not surprisingly, a society that hates these two things is a society that is very unhappy. It certainly does not want to hear the words, "Merry Christmas."

Therefore, let's not bother with the usual complaints about the commercialization of our sacred Christian feast. Let's not be offended when some poor wage slave wishes us a happy holiday. We know that the holiday is a holy day. But let's not quiver at the controversy. Let us roll up our sleeves and plunge in up to our elbows in the controversy! Let us controverse! Let us proclaim loud and clear: "Merry Christmas!" "For Unto Us a Child is Born!" "Tidings of Comfort and Joy." And blessed are those who take no offense at us. As for those who do take offense, let them be offended at our great joy. If they will not accept our tidings of comfort, let them make no mistake about our joy.

Chapter Fifty-Four

WHY PEOPLE DON'T GO TO CHURCH

When I was still a Protestant, at a certain point I stopped going to church. I had not lost interest in the Christian faith; I still considered it the most important thing in my life. But I had definitely lost interest in going to church. We never felt at home, and I finally figured out that there was nothing being done in any of them that we couldn't do at home. And so we stayed home and did "home church."

But it did not work. Something was missing. And during the week, when I was driving from one meeting to another, I found myself stopping at churches and going inside to pray. At first, I would stop at any church. But it was not long before the only churches I stopped at all had something in common: they were Catholic. There were two reasons for this: first, they were the only ones that were always open, and second, I noticed a "presence" there that I did not find anywhere else. I continued this secret life for a long time until the day I made the shocking announcement to my long-suffering wife that we had started going to church again on Sunday—and to a Catholic church! In the meantime, you see, I had been reading G.K. Chesterton, who convinced me that the thing I had been protesting against— the Catholic Church—was my true home. And I'd also been reading the Early Church Fathers, who convinced me that that presence I had sensed in the Catholic churches was none other than Christ Himself in the Eucharist. The Catholic Church had something to offer that I could not get at "home church." Or in any other church.

Chesterton once read a newspaper article entitled "The Empty Pews Can Be Filled," where some modern critic explored the reason why people don't go to church and what can be done to get them to go. After reading the suggestions, he was tempted to write a reply to all such critics entitled "These Empty Heads Can Be Filled."

What the critic was arguing was that religion needed to be freed from doctrine. Then people would come back to church. If the preachers would not focus so much on doctrine, they would be more popular. Doctrine was considered offensive and exclusive and stifling. What was needed was emancipation! But what the critic was calling emancipation was, according to Chesterton, emptiness. The criticism about doctrine was purely negative; the critic had nothing positive to offer in the place of the doctrine which upset him so.

Emptying sermons of doctrine does not fill the pews. Preaching something vague and inoffensive will not induce people to go to church. Even the Protestants have figured that out. The successful Protestant churches are not known for their milquetoast sermons. If there is one thing that they have proved it is that good strong preaching, the kind that separates the sheep from the goats, will pack the place. But the weakness of these churches is that they are almost entirely dependent on the personality of the preacher. Chesterton muses that it is ironic that the very Protestants who complain about the "theatricality" of the Catholic Church, were introducing all the elements of theater into their own worship services, from the music to the stage lighting, casting a rose halo on the preacher.

There was a time in Chesterton's life when he did not go to

church. He was an Anglican at the time. Was it the preaching that
kept him away? Would some Reverend who carefully avoided
the subject of God or of doctrines with which he did not agree
have deterred him from going for a walk or reading a detective
novel or simply staying in bed? Nope.

> Would I have got up early in the morning to go to church,
> merely because a good kind clergyman could be trusted to
> omit anything that was in any way orthodox? What do you
> think? I stayed away from church, as I imagine most of the
> jolly people nowadays do stay away from church, because
> I wanted to do something else or very much wanted to do
> nothing; not because I was afraid of being insulted in the holy
> edifice by the mention of the Incarnation or the Trinity. I did
> not want to hear dull heterodox sermons any more than dull
> orthodox sermons.

Chesterton goes on to say that the pews are empty because
the world is full; it is "full of all sorts of things which it is quite
natural to prefer to doing one's duty." And he argues that people
cannot be expected to give up these things in favor of their duty,
even for half an hour, if their duty is not clearly and rationally
explained to them and connected with some sort of solid philosophy about life. That is precisely what religion is supposed
to provide. We are not going to fill the churches with religious
people by preaching sermons emptied of religion. But while the
sermons would do well to have some substance to them, that
is still not the point of going to church.

Chesterton notes that "progressives" usually try to fix a
problem from the wrong end. Instead of going back to the
beginning to figure out how we have gone wrong, they look at
the mess we're in and simply try to figure out what to do next, to
progress, to move forward, not knowing what the goal is. Instead

of looking at the foundation of the Church, they are looking at empty pews. And they think the solution is to ignore what is written on the foundation stone. They avoid the big question. What is the meaning of the commandment about keeping the Sabbath? If it means simply work six days and rest on the seventh, we can do that by staying home. If it means everybody be nice to everybody else, we can also do that without going to church. But obviously it means something more. It is has to do with very act that instituted our faith: Christ's sacrifice at Calvary. That is why we have a crucifix hanging over the sanctuary. We go to Mass on Sunday because of what Christ Himself did at the beginning of the Passion, when he sat down with his beloved and began a chain of events that would lead to the salvation of all mankind. He initiated a regular commemoration of that event so that we might always be aware of it, so that there would be a way for us to be present at the moment when he took the bread and wine and said, "This is my body. This is my blood. Do this in remembrance of Me."

When the local Anglican vicar heard that Chesterton was going to convert, he said, "I'm glad he's becoming Catholic. He was never a very good Anglican."

After his conversion, Chesterton never missed a day of obligation. He said that only a religion that was true could have gotten him out of the bed that early in the morning.

Someone once asked me, "Do you really think it's a mortal sin to miss Mass?"

I answered with a question: "When Christ Himself has commanded: 'Do this in remembrance of me,' what excuse do you think is good enough to disobey Him?"

Chapter Fifty-Five

EVERYTHING PROVES IT

In *Orthodoxy*, his masterly defense of the Christian faith, G.K Chesterton writes: "It is very hard for a man to defend anything of which he is entirely convinced. It is comparatively easy when he is only partially convinced. He is partially convinced because he has found this or that proof of the thing, and he can expound it. But a man is not really convinced of a philosophic theory when he finds that something proves it. He is only really convinced when he finds that everything proves it."

Chesterton's point is born out any time someone asks the question, "How do you know the Catholic faith is true?" We have a difficult time coming up with an easy answer. There are so many things we could say that suddenly we can think of nothing to say. None of the answers we could give appear to be sufficient by themselves, but when taken together, they make a case for the faith that is hard to dispute. Indeed, it is not that one thing proves it; it is that everything proves it.

When we have our days of doubt, when we are confused by the incessant attacks and the personal disappointments, it is a good exercise to sit down and make a list of all the things that prove that the Catholic faith is true.

࿔ The Church is the only consistent defender of morality and virtue. It defends marriage and the family. It defends children and babies, including babies in the womb. It defends the poor. It defends human dignity. It defends order and it also defends freedom. It defends the body and the mind and the soul.

❧ The Church is the only institution in history that has continually survived its own defeats, even, as Chesterton says, its own death. Several times in history the Church seemed to be done and destroyed. But it is still here. It has survived its own death, says Chesterton, "because it had a God who knew his way out of the grave."

❧ The history of Christianity is the history of the Catholic Church. The Church has not only carried the faith through history, it has carried the whole culture. The monasteries preserved the texts of the ancient world, keeping open our only windows to the past. When iconoclasts were smashing statues, Catholics preserved the art of sculpture. Catholic artists even brought sculpture inside paintings, giving them depth and dimension. They wrote music that we can still sing. The castles built in the medieval times are now museums or ruins. The Cathedrals built at the same time are still Cathedrals.

❧ All other Christian sects are a reaction against or a splitting off from the Catholic Church. They are always something less than the Catholic Church, never anything more. They lack something, whether it is a pope or a priest or a pronouncement. Whatever partial truth they cling to is something that they have received from the Catholic Church, whether it be the Bible or baptism or "bringing in the sheaves." As Chesterton says, the Catholic Church is the only church that can dare call itself "The Church."

❧ History's greatest people, the saints, are Catholic. We too often forget how great they are. They have worked miracles, they have defied unbelievable odds, they have written monumental testimonies of truth, they have had exquisite visions, they have suffered unimaginable hardship with unexplainable joy, they have selflessly served their fellow human beings, caring for the sick and the dying and the outcast with astonishing charity. They have willingly died for their faith rather than live without it. There may be outstanding individuals in history who did one thing well or lived notable and worthy lives: Buddha, Confucius, Spinoza, Gandhi, Martin Luther King and so on. But whomever you want to name, not one of them, *not one of them*, compares with the smallest saint, with St. Maria Goretti, with the Little Flower, with Don Bosco, with St. Francis de Sales, with Blessed Miriam Baouardy, with Mother Teresa. One saint is enough to prove the truth of the Church. But we have hundreds and every one of them lived an exemplary life worth contemplating and imitating.

☙ Even the sins of the Catholic Church are evidence of its truth. Its failures only point to the great value of its precepts. The world cannot abide the Church failing because the world unconsciously knows that the truth it proclaims must be upheld. Chesterton says that the sins of Christianity are one of the doctrines of Christianity. In other words, our sins point to one of our sacraments: confession. He says, "The Church is not justified when her children do not sin, but when they do."

The list goes on. We can always add to it. There is always another reason to believe the Church's teachings, always more evidence to support its truth. As Chesterton says, the Church "has endured for two thousand years; and the world within the Church has been more lucid, more level-headed, more reasonable in its hopes, more healthy in its instincts, more humorous and cheerful in the face of fate and death, than all the world outside."

Everything proves it.

꒰♦

Chapter Fifty-Six

ROME

It is possible to visit the same place and yet visit two completely different places.

The first time I visited Rome, I was a tourist. I was also a Baptist. I was also reading my first Chesterton book. And just to affirm what is already on record, I was also on my honeymoon. Rome was an exciting and exotic place for me, obviously carrying the weight of history and stuffed full of stunning art and architecture. Even though the sculpture was a wonder to behold, some of those statues seemed to be serving questionable purposes for my tastes. I am not talking about the pagan ones. I am talking about the religious ones. I am talking about the way pilgrims knelt in front of Mary and fondled the foot of Peter. It was crossing the line from art appreciation to, well, idolatry. Or so I presumed.

Twenty-five years later I visited Rome again. This time I was not a tourist. I was a pilgrim. And a Catholic. It was the same place, except that it was completely different. I saw the city with a new set of eyes. The buildings were no longer "architecture." They were churches. The statues were no longer "art." They were testimonies in stone.

Since I was there only a few days, I visited only about 20 of Rome's 400 churches. And I saw only a small portion of that huge population of marble figures who dwell in those churches and stand guard all along the streets. In a city where there seem to be as many churches as houses, as many statues as people, where each building, each carving is a masterpiece, there is still one special place where the churches and statues come together like nowhere else on earth. That place is St. Peter's Basilica.

A fellow Catholic convert of mine walked into St. Peter's about 70 years before I did, and he, too, saw how this church is different from every other church on earth. That fellow was G.K. Chesterton. He says that although there are churches and shrines all over the world in which people can realize their own insignificance in the presence of Jesus Christ, here is the Rock of Offense. Here is the place where a very grand claim is made: that there is someone among us who possesses a special warrant from Christ Himself. That is the meaning of the Vicar of Christ.

According to Chesterton there are two main ideas associated with St. Peter's, and if you don't understand these two ideas, you don't understand what the place is all about. The two ideas are Certitude and the Spoken Word, which happen to be precisely the two ideas that I did not understand on my first visit and that I did understand on my second visit.

Certitude and the Spoken Word are epitomized by the many statues. If architecture is frozen music, statues are frozen rhetoric. All the statues have the certitude of rock, and they have the pose of the spoken word. They are all preaching. They proclaim in stone "the intolerant and intolerable notion that something is really true; true in every aspect and from every angle; true from the four quarters of the sky; true by the three dimensions of the Trinity." The statues stand for a fullness of Truth that can be approached from all sides. The statues are marble that has symbolically (and incredibly realistically) been turned into flesh, because God himself literally became flesh. And the statues stand as witnesses around all the altars of that place, where every day bread is turned into flesh. Christ's prophecy is fulfilled: the stones cry out.

Certitude and the Spoken Word. Those are two ideas that the world cannot abide. The world, which so often calls the Church intolerant, is itself intolerant of the Church. Because the world cannot stand a religion that is not only sure of itself but says so. The world cannot stand the Catholic Church because it makes clear and confident statements about what is right and what is wrong, about what is true and what is false, about what is authority and what is defiance.

The world falls into the fallacy that freedom exists apart from the rules. The truth is precisely the other way around. Freedom is in obedience, not disobedience. Freedom exists only within the rules. As Chesterton says, Catholic doctrine and discipline may be walls, but they are the walls of a playground.

The rules are few. In following them we are free. In breaking them we are enslaved. The problem is we are always looking for a way around the rules. We are always looking for an exception. And if we occasionally find an exception, we are soon emphasizing the exceptions, and not the rules. And then, suddenly, there are no rules, only exceptions. This has led to the modern problem that Chesterton enunciated perfectly: "The exception has become the rule, and that is the worst of all possible tyrannies."

This line, written in 1914, exactly anticipates the words of the Cardinal formerly known as Ratzinger in his last homily before he was elected Pope. He said that we are living under the dictatorship of relativism. Relativism is what happens when there are no rules, only exceptions, when the exception becomes the rule. Relativism is tyranny. And tyranny is the enemy of freedom. Freedom only exists within the rules.

The Catholic Church is founded on a rock. The fashions of

the world, the events of history, the changing philosophies of the ages all swirl around it, but the Church remains solid and steady and unmoving. Like a rock. And though the Church is old, it always seems new, because its truths always refresh us, while the new ideas fail to satisfy and fade quickly, the urgencies are gone before they arrive. Fads always have a desperate character to them. Traditions are always steady and patient. That is because, as Chesterton says, a tradition is a living thing, not a dead one.

But there is more to it. Much more. It is not just a matter of the traditions surviving as the fashions fail and fade. It is something more profound. It is the dead coming to life. It is resurrection. We worship the God who knows his way out of the grave.

That is why it is fitting that Rome is a city full of tombs, but full of life.

And just as fittingly, it is a city full of fountains. Chesterton noted that the fountains which are everywhere in Rome are a perfect symbol of the city. They are a paradox: water running uphill. Something hidden emerging from below. The buried things do not remain buried. Rome is a city of resurrection; it is not a place where one returns to the past, but where the past returns to the present. Where even the future is mystically drawn into the present. It is the Eternal City because it is the open window to the Kingdom of Heaven.

My journey to Rome began in Rome. It was the place I left in order to find my way back. But it meant actually turning around. All roads lead to Rome. But that means that all roads also lead away from Rome. It does not matter which road we are on, but we are either traveling toward the Church or away from it. Those are the only two choices. *Quo Vadis?*

THE END